Discovering Food and Nutrition

STUDENT WORKBOOK

Fifth Edition

Connie R. Sasse, CFCS

Glencoe
McGraw-Hill

New York, New York   Columbus, Ohio   Woodland Hills, California   Peoria, Illinois

Illustrators: Erica Coker
Angela Crouser

Glencoe/McGraw-Hill

A Division of The **McGraw·Hill** *Companies*

Send all inquires to:
Glencoe/McGraw-Hill
3008 W. Willow Knolls Drive
Peoria, IL   61614-1083

ISBN 0-02-642908-X

Printed in the United States of America

5 6 7 8 9 10 11 12   069   02 01 00

CONTENTS

UNIT ONE: LOOKING AHEAD

Chapter 1: The Adventure of Food
Study Guide 9
Short- and Long-term Goals 11
A Puzzling Adventure 12

Chapter 2: Managing Your Resources
Study Guide 13
Resource Match Ups 15
Linda's Decision 16

Chapter 3: What About Careers?
Study Guide 17
Job Skills 19
Decipher the Code 20

UNIT TWO: NUTRITION

Chapter 4: Wellness—Your Goal for Life
Study Guide 21
A Wellness Plan for José 23
Magic Wellness Square 24

Chapter 5: How Nutrients Work for You
Study Guide 25
Nutrient Match Up 27
Puzzling Over Nutrients 28
A Healthy Diet 30

Chapter 6: What Are Food Guides?
Study Guide 31
Food Groups and Nutrients 33
Hidden Foods 34

Chapter 7: Making Healthful Food Choices
Study Guide 35
"Souper" Salads 37
The Key to Food Choices 38

UNIT THREE: DEVELOPING SKILLS

Chapter 8: Shopping for Food
Study Guide 39
Unit Pricing 41
Grocery Shopping 42

Chapter 9: Using Kitchen Appliances
Study Guide 43
Identifying Small Appliances 45
What Are the Consequences? 46

Chapter 10: Know Your Equipment
Study Guide 47
Identifying Equipment 49
Equipment Crossword 50
What Equipment Is Needed? 52

Chapter 11: Reading Recipes
Study Guide 53
Understanding the Recipe 55
Magic Terms Square 56

Chapter 12: Recipe Math
Study Guide 57
Measuring Match Ups 59
Hidden Measurements 60
Looking at Equivalents 62

Chapter 13: Basic Measuring Methods
Study Guide 63
Choosing Measuring Methods 65
Recipe Measuring 66

Chapter 14: Basic Cooking Methods
Study Guide 67
Hidden Cooking Terms 69
Actions and Consequences 70

Chapter 15: Microwave Techniques
Study Guide 71
Microwave Countdown 73
The Microwave File 74

UNIT FOUR: GOOD WORK HABITS

Chapter 16: Safety in the Kitchen
Study Guide 75
Safety Errors 77
Safe or Unsafe? 78
What's the Word? 80

Chapter 17: Keeping Food Safe to Eat
Study Guide 81
Food Storage 83
Food Safety 84

Chapter 18: Getting Organized
Study Guide 85
Planning Ahead 87
Kitchen Code 88

Chapter 19: Conserving and Recycling
Study Guide 89
Conserving and Recycling 91
Conserve Your Resources 92

UNIT FIVE: MEALTIME

Chapter 20: Meal Management
Study Guide 93
Meal Manager 95
Call for Successful Meal Planning 96

Chapter 21: Serving a Meal
Study Guide 97
Hidden Tableware 99
Place Settings 100

Chapter 22: Packing a Lunch
Study Guide 101
Annie's Advice 103
Magic Lunch Square 104

UNIT SIX: LEARNING ABOUT FOODS

Chapter 23: Milk
Study Guide 105
Milk Match Ups 107
Cooking with Milk 108

Chapter 24: Yogurt and Cheese
Study Guide 109
Cheese Clues 111
What Would You Buy? 112

Chapter 25: Grain Products
Study Guide 113
Grains and Breads Puzzle 115
Reading Cereal Labels 116
Cooking Grain Products 118

Chapter 26: Fruits
Study Guide 119
Choosing Nutritious Fruits 121
Consumer Power 123

Chapter 27: Vegetables
Study Guide 125
Find the Veggies 127
Steps to a Perfect Vegetable Tray 128

Chapter 28: Legumes
Study Guide 129
Legume Magic Square 131
Legume Calculations 132

Chapter 29: Poultry
Study Guide 133
Telephone Terms 135
Poultry Math 136

Chapter 30: Fish and Shellfish
Study Guide 137
Fishy Calculating 139
Hidden Fish and Shellfish 140

Chapter 31: Meat
Study Guide 141
How Much Does a Serving Cost? 143
Meat Puzzler 144
Look at the Label 146

Chapter 32: Eggs
Study Guide 147
Buying Eggs 149
The Key to Egg Cookery 150

UNIT SEVEN: CREATIVE COMBINATIONS

Chapter 33: Salads
Study Guide 151
A Tossed Salad 153
Mystery Salad 154

Chapter 34: Soups
Study Guide 155
Soup Savvy 157
Soup Match Ups 158

Chapter 35: One-Dish Meals
Study Guide 159
Scrambled Ingredients 161
Crossword Puzzle 162
Designer Pizza 164

Chapter 36: Snacks
Study Guide 165
Vending Machine Choices 167
Healthful Snacks 168

Chapter 37: Beverages
Study Guide 169
Where's the Juice? 171
Coded Messages 172

UNIT EIGHT: BAKING

Chapter 38: Principles of Baking
Study Guide 173
A File for Baking 175
Analyzing Recipe Ingredients 177
Preparing to Bake 179
STEPS to Baking Success 180

Chapter 39: Quick Breads
Study Guide 181
Mixing Methods 183
Quick Bread Combinations 184

Chapter 40: Cookies, Cakes, and Pies
Study Guide 185
Problem Solvers 187
Hidden Treats 189
Sweet Treat Match Ups 191

Study Guide

Completion: In the space to the left, write the word or words that **BEST** complete(s) each statement.

_____ 1. In this course you will study food and ___?___.

_____ 2. Meals as well as ___?___ should be nutritious and delicious.

_____ 3. You will look and feel your best if you eat a(n) ___?___ of nutritious foods each day.

_____ 4. People who eat a variety of food each day are more likely to be more ___?___ and active than those who don't.

_____ 5. One fun part of cooking is trying different food ___?___, that is, putting several kinds of food together.

_____ 6. You will be able to use basic food ___?___ skills throughout your life.

_____ 7. Some of the skills you will need are reading, writing, and basic __?___.

_____ 8. One advantage of studying food in school is learning to work together as a ___?___.

_____ 9. The study of food will help you know how to ___?___ and prepare meals.

_____ 10. Selecting foods and preparing them will help you develop new or reinforce old ___?___.

_____ 11. One way to help you see what you want to accomplish is to set ___?___.

_____ 12. A task to be accomplished in the near future is a(n) ___?___ goal.

_____ 13. One example of a goal would be to prepare a whole nutritious, delicious ___?___ for your family.

_____ 14. A task to be accomplished sometime in the far future is a(n) ___?___ goal.

_____ 15. It takes time and ___?___ to become skilled at food preparation.

_____ 16. Accomplishing goals proves to yourself that you can be ___?___.

_____ 17. Believing in your ability to succeed is known as ___?___.

Continued on next page

_____ 18. Learning from your ___?___ will help you become skilled at food preparation.

Short Answer: Answer the following questions on the lines provided.

19. Why is it an advantage to know how to prepare many different foods?

_____

_____

20. What are four ways you will be able to use food preparation skills?

_____

_____

21. What are two advantages of setting goals?

_____

_____

22. How are long- and short-term goals similar and different? Give an example of each.

_____

_____

23. Describe three short-term goals that will help you accomplish the long-term goal of fixing a meal for your friends.

_____

_____

_____

24. What is involved in becoming skillful in food preparation?

_____

_____

25. How can you measure your progress as you practice preparing food?

_____

_____

Name _____ **Date** _____ **Class Hour** _____

CHAPTER **1** The Adventure of Food

  ▼ ## Short- and Long-Term Goals

Directions: Read the goals listed below. Write "short" in the blank to the left of the goal if it is a short-term goal. Write "long" in the blank to the left of the goal if it is a long-term one.

_____ 1. Sue wants to lose two pounds by this Friday.

_____ 2. Bob hopes to get at least a B on his foods test this class period.

_____ 3. Gwen is saving her money for a compact disc player.

_____ 4. Juanita wants to become an engineer.

_____ 5. Emily plans to go buy new eye make-up after school.

_____ 6. Brandon wants to learn to make pizza from scratch in his foods class.

_____ 7. Paul plans to visit his grandmother this weekend.

_____ 8. Carla wants to attend the local community college when she graduates from high school.

_____ 9. Joe is going to pick up groceries after school tonight.

_____ 10. Andrea has to pick up her softball uniform from her manager before the first game next week.

_____ 11. David wants to raise his free-throw percentage to 75 percent before the end of the basketball season.

_____ 12. Margo wants to work as a supermarket checker next summer.

_____ 13. Bo hopes to earn an A in his foods class this semester.

_____ 14. Lori plans to attend the football game this Friday night.

_____ 15. Kym Lee is saving money for a car of his own.

CHAPTER 1 The Adventure of Food   **Text Pages 8-11**

 A Puzzling Adventure

Directions: Listed below are clues that have to do with the adventure of food. Use each clue to complete the blank spaces in the corresponding numbered item.

1. ____ **A** ____ ____ ____ ____

2. ____ ____ ____ ____ ____ **D** ____ ____ ____ ____

3. ____ ____ ____ ____ **V** ____

4. ____ **E** ____ ____

5. ____ ____ **N** ____ - ____ ____ ____ ____

6. ____ ____ ____ ____ **T** ____ ____ ____

7. ____ **U** ____ ____ ____ ____ ____ ____ ____

8. ____ ____ ____ ____ **R** ____ - ____ ____ ____ ____

9. ____ ____ ____ ____ **E** ____

Clues

1. The study of foods could lead to this in foods.

2. Having this in yourself means you believe you will succeed.

3. Nutritious foods will help keep you in this condition.

4. You will work as a part of this in the foods laboratory.

5. A goal to accomplish far in the future.

6. What it will take to master food preparation skills.

7. This will be a part of your study in foods class.

8. A goal to be accomplished in the near future.

9. This is what a goal is like.

Study Guide

Completion: In the space to the left, write the word or words that **BEST** complete(s) each statement.

_____ 1. Something you can use to reach your goals is called a(n) ___?___.

_____ 2. ___?___ is using your resources wisely to meet your goals.

_____ 3. People who have lots of ___?___ can accomplish more.

_____ 4. The knowledge and ___?___ you have learned are valuable personal resources.

_____ 5. Being creative and solving problems is related to the resource of ___?___.

_____ 6. Possessions that are seen and touched are ___?___ resources.

_____ 7. An important resource for staying healthy is ___?___.

_____ 8. Useful objects that help you make or prepare things are ___?___.

_____ 9. The resources that are based in other people are ___?___ resources.

_____ 10. Materials provided by nature are called ___?___ resources.

_____ 11. When your friend learns a new skill, ___?___ resources are increased.

_____ 12. The best way to manage resources that are in short supply is ___?___.

_____ 13. Using resources wisely instead of wasting them is practicing ___?___.

_____ 14. Conservation is especially important for ___?___ resources.

_____ 15. One way to manage resources is to ___?___ one for another.

_____ 16. The first step in making a decision is to ___?___ the problem.

_____ 17. Next, you should consider what ___?___ are available.

_____ 18. In thinking of different ways to solve a problem, you are comparing the ___?___.

_____ 19. In addition to coming up with a plan you must ___?___ it out.

_____ 20. To judge how well you met a goal is to ___?___ the results.

Continued on next page

Short Answer: Answer the following questions on the lines provided.

21. What are the four kinds of resources? Why is it important to know what resources you have available?

_____

_____

22. What are three kinds of social resources?

_____

_____

_____

23. What kinds of help can social resources provide for you?

_____

_____

_____

24. What are five examples of resources in your community?

_____

_____

25. What are four examples of natural resources?

_____

_____

26. What are some ways that you can use resources wisely?

_____

_____

27. Give an example of how one resource can be substituted for another.

_____

_____

_____

28. What factors should you consider when comparing options in making decisions?

_____

_____

_____

Name _____   Date _____   Class Hour_____

CHAPTER 2 Managing Your Resources   **Text Pages 12-15**

  ## Resource Match Ups

Directions: Match each resource in the left column with the correct type of resource from the right column. Write the letter of the type of resource in the space provided. Each type of resource will be used at least once.

Resource	**Type of Resource**
____ 1. A free afternoon	A. Material resource
____ 2. Fuel to heat the house in winter	B. Natural resource
____ 3. A $20 bill for your birthday	C. Personal resource
____ 4. A softball and bat	D. Social resource
____ 5. A best friend	
____ 6. The ability to change oil in a car	
____ 7. A park across the street	
____ 8. The energy to run three miles	
____ 9. The local library	
____ 10. A dishwasher	
____ 11. Fresh water in the tap	
____ 12. A home to live in	
____ 13. Support from parents	
____ 14. Gasoline to run the car	
____ 15. Skills to make pillows and curtains	

CHAPTER 2 Managing Your Resources   **Text Pages 12-15**

▼ ▼ ▼ Linda's Decision

   Linda has decided to treat her friend Maria to dinner on Maria's birthday. Maria really likes Mexican food and enjoys going to the Mexican Fiesta Restaurant. Linda would like to take her there, but she doesn't have enough money. She would have to borrow some money to pay for the dinner. Linda knows how to make tacos, nachos, and enchiladas. She thinks she has enough money to buy the ingredients to cook a birthday dinner for Maria. However, she's afraid making dinner for Maria at home won't seem very festive. Use the steps in the decision-making process to help Linda make her choice. Write your answers to the questions below on the lines provided.

1. What exactly is the decision Linda is trying to make?

   _____

   _____

2. What are Linda's resources?

   _____

   _____

3. What options does Linda have?

   _____

   _____

4. What are the good and bad points of each option?

   _____

   _____

5. Which option do you think Linda should choose? Why?

   _____

   _____

6. How will Linda know whether she made the right choice?

   _____

   _____

CHAPTER 3 **What About Careers**    **Text Pages 16-21**

Study Guide

Completion: In the space to the left, write the word or words that **BEST** complete(s) each statement.

_____ 1. The work you choose to do for a long period of time or in a specific field is called a(n) ___?___.

_____ 2. Being ___?___ means following through on assignments.

_____ 3. Being willing to ___?___ will be important throughout your life.

_____ 4. Listening, speaking, reading, and writing are good ___?___ skills.

_____ 5. Filling out a time card or running a cash register requires basic ___?___ skills.

_____ 6. ___?___ is a skill that will help you work together with others to achieve a specific goal.

_____ 7. Employers look for people who are willing to do their ___?___ of the work.

_____ 8. Food service workers may use ___?___ to develop and store recipes.

_____ 9. Participating in school ___?___ or committees can help you learn skills useful on the job.

_____ 10. Personal ___?___ and enjoyment are benefits that can be provided by work.

_____ 11. It is important to find a career that fits your abilities, personality, family life, goals, and ___?___.

_____ 12. A person who can help you think and find out about different careers is a(n) ___?___.

_____ 13. A(n) ___?___ job is one that does not require experience or a college degree.

_____ 14. Higher paying jobs are available to those with more training and ___?___.

_____ 15. Workers in the ___?___ industry provide meals purchased and eaten away from home.

_____ 16. An example of a beginning job in food service is one at a(n) ___?___ restaurant.

_____ 17. People who help others develop healthful eating habits are called ___?___.

Continued on next page

_____ 18. Food specialists who develop new products, test chemicals, or make discoveries about nutrition are called ___?___.

_____ 19. Plants are grown in water instead of soil in ___?___ farming.

_____ 20. Food that is ready for sale has been ___?___.

_____ 21. Before it is packaged, food must be ___?___ for quality.

_____ 22. The person who directs and coordinates all activities of the supermarket is the ___?___.

Short Answer: Answer the following questions on the lines provided.

23. Why is the "willingness to learn" a skill you will need your whole life?

_____

_____

24. Give examples of how you might use the four basic communication skills on the job.

_____

_____

25. What are three characteristics of a responsible worker?

_____

_____

26. List at least three ways that you and the work you choose to do should fit.

_____

_____

_____

27. List at least five different places where food service workers may be employed.

_____

_____

_____

28. What is the overall purpose of careers in food production and marketing?

_____

_____

29. What are two entry-level jobs in a supermarket? Even though no training is necessary for this type of job, what personal abilities would be helpful?

_____

_____

Job Skills

Directions: The list below on the left describes various on-the-job activities of some of the people who work in a supermarket. Decide what ability listed in the right column is shown by the employee and write the letter of the ability shown in the blank to the left of the activity described.

Activities on the Job

_____ 1. Josie and Kelly worked together to refill the frozen food case.

_____ 2. Jeff has been asked to learn the new computer program the store is purchasing.

_____ 3. David refilled the copy machine when it ran out of paper.

_____ 4. Meg added the receipts from six cash drawers at the end of the shift.

_____ 5. Drew wrote a report explaining the advantages of installing an automatic sprinkling system in the produce department.

_____ 6. Bonita figured and made the bank deposit each day.

_____ 7. Bob talked to Kelly and told her unless she started coming in on time for her shift, she would be fired.

_____ 8. David accidentally left some pallets outside one night and the next day they were gone. He told his boss about it and offered to pay for the missing pallets.

_____ 9. When the store bought new cash registers, all the checkers were trained to use them.

_____ 10. Meg was assigned to work with the Downtown Merchants Association to plan a holiday promotion for Halloween.

_____ 11. Part of Jeff's job is to deal with customers who have complaints.

_____ 12. Becka adds up the employees hours each week so their paychecks can be written.

Abilities Shown by Employees

A. Willingness to learn

B. Good communication skills

C. Basic math skills

D. Teamwork

E. Responsibility

CHAPTER 3 What About Careers   **Text Pages 16-21**

 Decipher the Code

Directions: The following sentences contain coded terms from the chapter. Use the example and definitions to break the code. Decode the mystery message in number 9.

Example: W O R K   A N D   Y O U
           N F I B   R E U   P F L

1. Many __ __ __ __ __ - __ __ __ __ __ jobs are in fast food restaurants.
          V E K I P   C V M V C

2. Some food service workers take __ __ __ __ __ __ at a counter.
                                    F I U V I J

3. Many food service workers are employed in schools, __ __ __ __ __ __ __ __ __ , or nursing homes.
                                                        Y F J G Z K R C J

4. Some __ __ __ __ __ __ __ __ __ __ __ __ __ help families stay within their budgets while choosing
         E L K I Z K Z F E Z J K J
healthful foods.

5. __ __ __ __ __ __ __ __ __ __ __ __ __ __ __ __ teachers help students learn good consumer practices.
   W F F U   R E U   E L K I Z K Z F E

6. Methods of __ __ __ __ __ __ __ __ __ __ food are packaging, canning, and freezing.
               G I F T V J J Z E X

7. Selling food is part of a food __ __ __ __ __ __ __ __ __ career.
                                   D R I B V K Z E X

8. Some people write about and __ __ __ __ __ __ __ __ __ __ food.
                                G Y F K F X I R G Y

9. __ __ __ __ __ __ __ __ __ __ __ __ __ __ __ __ __ __ __ __
   K Y V I V   R I V   D R E P   V O T Z K Z E X

   __ __ __ __ __ __ __ __ __ __ __ __ __ __ __ __ __ __ __ __ __ __ __ __ .
   T R I V V I J   Z E   K Y V   W F F U   Z E U L J K I P

Discovering Food and Nutrition Student Workbook Protected by Copyright ©

Study Guide

Completion: In the space to the left, write the word or words that **BEST** complete(s) each statement.

_____ 1. Having good ___?___, ___?___, and ___?___ health is known as wellness.

_____

_____

_____ 2. Taking ___?___ for your own health is also part of wellness.

_____ 3. In the years to come, your ___?___ will be affected by the health habits you establish now.

_____ 4. Eating ___?___ food is part of a wellness plan.

_____ 5. Chemicals that the body needs to work properly are called ___?___.

_____ 6. Even when you are sleeping, your body needs the ___?___ that nutrients help provide.

_____ 7. When the body grows, it builds new ___?___.

_____ 8. Nutrients are important in ___?___ body processes.

_____ 9. Waste products built up in the muscles each day are gotten rid of in ___?___.

_____ 10. When people are ___?___ they need extra sleep.

_____ 11. Exercise is important in firming and toning ___?___.

_____ 12. Muscles become ___?___ when they work hard at pushing or pulling.

_____ 13. You develop flexibility when you do ___?___ exercises.

_____ 14. To continue a physical activity for a long time requires ___?___.

_____ 15. ___?___ exercises help the body take in and use more oxygen.

_____ 16. Physical and emotional tension is called ___?___.

_____ 17. Stress that is out of control affects your ___?___ and ___?___.

_____ 18. A ___?___ attitude that lets a person look for the good can help control stress.

Continued on next page

_____ 19. Physical activity is one way to work off ___?___.

_____ 20. Cancer, heart disease, and lung disease have all been linked to ___?___.

_____ 21. A major cause of auto accidents is ___?___ and driving.

_____ 22. The use of ___?___ interferes with work and school.

_____ 23. The best age to develop good health habits is while you are ___?___.

Short Answer: Answer the following questions on the lines provided.

24. Give at least three examples of body processes that are regulated by nutrients.

_____

_____

25. Why do teens need more sleep than adults?

_____

_____

26. How does a person know if he or she is getting enough sleep?

_____

_____

27. How does aerobic exercise differ from stretching exercises?

_____

_____

28. What's the difference between strength, flexibility, and endurance? Give one specific exercise you could do to improve in each of these areas.

_____

_____

29. What is a positive advantage of stress?

_____

_____

30. Why is alcohol such a dangerous drug to take?

_____

_____

31. What kind of help can a health professional give in developing a wellness plan?

_____

_____

CHAPTER 4 **Wellness — Your Goal for Life**   **Text Pages 22-27**

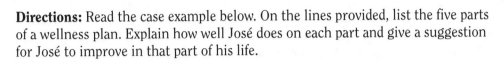 A Wellness Plan for José

Directions: Read the case example below. On the lines provided, list the five parts of a wellness plan. Explain how well José does on each part and give a suggestion for José to improve in that part of his life.

José wants to major in pharmacology (far-MUH-kahl-uh-jee) when he goes to college. His parents put a lot of emphasis on getting good grades so he can attend a good college. José worries about his grades and works hard to earn Bs and As. José is a good athlete. He plays basketball and baseball. However, he enjoys the time off between seasons because he doesn't have to exercise at all. José is often tired during the day but becomes more alert after dinner. He stays up late most nights watching television, talking on the phone, and relaxing. He sleeps too late to eat breakfast in the morning, so he is really hungry at lunch. He usually has two burgers, french fries, some dessert, and a large soft drink.

José's group of friends have a lot of fun together. However, lately, a couple of guys have gotten beer some weekends. So far, José hasn't had any, but he knows the time is coming when he may feel pressured by his friends to drink. He wonders if he will be able to say no.

The school Valentine's Dance is coming soon and José would like to ask Cindy, a girl in his math class. He doesn't know her very well and is afraid she'll say no. Every day he works to get his courage up to ask her, but finds himself tongue-tied and ends up not asking.

1. _____

_____

2. _____

_____

3. _____

_____

_____

_____

4. _____

_____

5. _____

_____

CHAPTER 4 **Wellness — Your Goal for Life**   **Text Pages 22-27**

Magic Wellness Square

Directions: Find the term which best fits each description. Write the number of the correct term in the space in each lettered square. If all your answers are correct, the total of the number, or the "Magic Number," will be the same in each row across and down. Write the Magic Number in the space provided.

Terms

1. body processes

2. aerobic activity

3. wellness

4. exercise

5. nutrients

6. sleep

7. alcohol

8. endurance

9. stress

10. tobacco

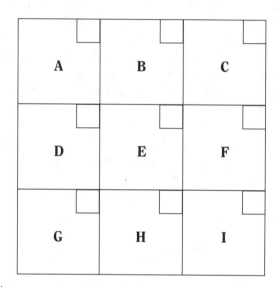

The Magic Number is _____.

Descriptions

A. Ability to continue physical activity for a long time.
B. Good physical, emotional, and mental health.
C. Activity to firm and tone muscles.
D. Time to rid the body of waste products in the muscles.
E. Can affect reactions and judgements.
F. Helps body take in and use more oxygen.
G. Needs good nutrition to happen continuously.
H. Chemicals in food that help the body work properly.
I. Emotional and physical tension.

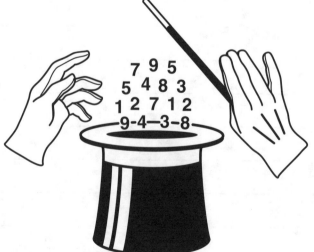

Name _____   **Date** _____   **Class Hour** _____

Study Guide

Completion: In the space to the left, write the word or words that **BEST** complete(s) each statement.

_____ 1. During ___?___, the body breaks down food into liquid.

_____ 2. ___?___ and ___?___ are examples of carbohydrates.

_____

_____ 3. Carbohydrates come mainly from ___?___ foods.

_____ 4. Another name for sugars is ___?___ carbohydrates.

_____ 5. Starches are also called ___?___ carbohydrates.

_____ 6. Substances needed to build and repair body cells are ___?___.

_____ 7. The building blocks of protein are called ___?___.

_____ 8. The nine amino acids the body does not make are called ___?___ because the body must get them from food.

_____ 9. Foods with all the amino acids in the right amounts are ___?___ proteins.

_____ 10. Foods that lack one or more essential amino acids are called ___?___ proteins.

_____ 11. A fat-like substance made by the body is ___?___.

_____ 12. Foods from ___?___ are the only source of cholesterol.

_____ 13. Fats that are solid at room temperature are ___?___ fats.

_____ 14. Fats that are liquid at room temperature are ___?___ fats.

_____ 15. Vitamins A and D are examples of ___?___-soluble vitamins.

_____ 16. ___?___-soluble vitamins are not stored in the body.

_____ 17. The minerals ___?___ and ___?___ work together to build strong bones and teeth.

_____

_____ 18. The mineral needed so that the red blood cells can carry oxygen is ___?___.

_____ 19. Plant materials that don't break down in digestion are called ___?___.

_____ 20. A healthy digestive system requires ___?___ fiber such as wheat bran.

Continued on next page

Short Answer: Answer the following questions on the lines provided.

21. Explain why health experts suggest eating only small amounts of simple carbohydrates and large amounts of complex carbohydrates.

_____

_____

_____

22. How can you get complete protein from plant foods?

_____

_____

23. Why is some fat needed for good health?

_____

_____

24. What is the difference between fat-soluble and water-soluble vitamins?

_____

_____

_____

25. What role do copper, iodine, selenium, and zinc play in the body?

_____

_____

_____

26. Why does the body need water each day?

_____

_____

27. What are the Recommended Dietary Allowances (RDA)?

_____

_____

28. When are nutrient supplements a waste of money?

_____

_____

Discovering Food and Nutrition Student Workbook Protected by Copyright ©

CHAPTER **5** How Nutrients Work for You

   ## Nutrient Match Up

Directions: Match each nutrient function in the left column with the correct nutrient from the right column. Write the letter of the nutrient in the space provided. Each nutrient will be used at least once.

Nutrient Functions

_____ 1. Cushions vital organs

_____ 2. Provides energy for the body

_____ 3. Builds new cell

_____ 4. Heals wounds

_____ 5. Repairs injured cells

_____ 6. Keeps a normal heart beat

_____ 7. Keeps skin healthy

_____ 8. Keeps nerves and muscles healthy

_____ 9. Helps fight off disease

_____ 10. Insulates body from heat and cold

_____ 11. Promotes good vision

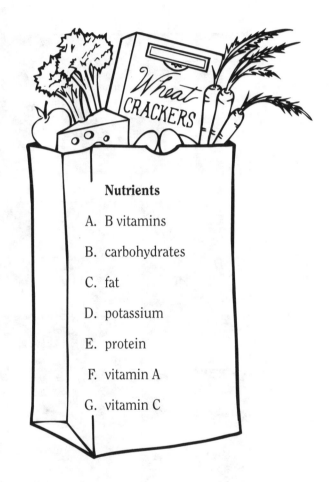

Nutrients

A. B vitamins

B. carbohydrates

C. fat

D. potassium

E. protein

F. vitamin A

G. vitamin C

CHAPTER 5 **How Nutrients Work for You** **Text Pages 28-35**

 Puzzling Over Nutrients

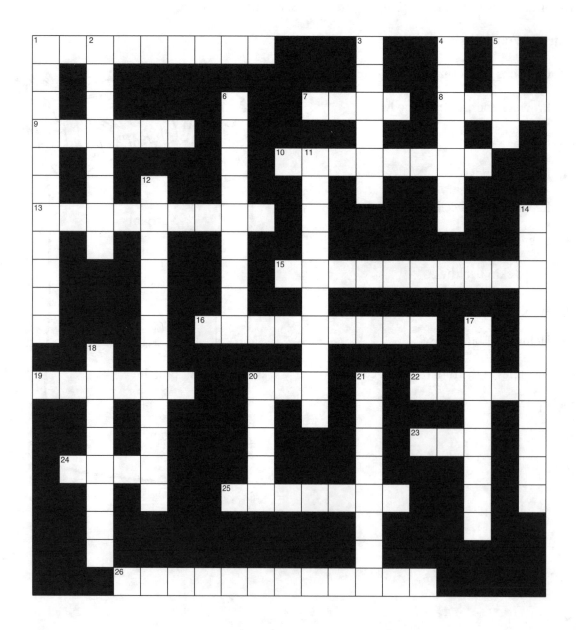

Continued on next page

Discovering Food and Nutrition Student Workbook Protected by Copyright ©

CHAPTER 5 How Nutrients Work for You   **Text Pages 28-35**

 Puzzling Over Nutrients

Directions: Fill in the crossword puzzle by placing the answer to each clue in the appropriate space.

Across

1. Fats that are solid at room temperature.
7. A source of fiber.
8. A food that contains natural sugars.
9. Proteins from this are incomplete.
10. Nutrients used for many body processes.
13. An example of a mineral.
15. Protein is made of these.
16. Type of fiber needed for good digestion.
19. A type of food high in complex carbohydrate.
20. Nutrient needed for healthy skin and insulation.
22. The body can live for only a few days without this.
23. A food high in added sugar.
24. A type of food with complete protein.
25. Nutrient that repairs body cells.
26. A kind of oil that has been turned into a solid fat.

Down

1. Pills, powders, or liquids that contain nutrients.
2. An example of a B vitamin.
3. An example of fat.
4. Type of carbohydrate found in starch.
5. An example of a saturated oil.
6. The process of breaking down food in the body.
11. Proteins that lack one or more of the essential amino acids.
12. The body's main source of energy.
14. Fats that are liquid at room temperature.
17. Nutrients that help other nutrients work properly.
18. Protein is needed to make these in the body.
20. Plant material that does not break down during digestion.
21. A chemical the body needs to work properly.

CHAPTER 5 How Nutrients Work for You **Text Pages 28-35**

 A Healthy Diet

Directions: Listed below are clues that relate to a healthy diet. Use each clue to complete the blank spaces in the corresponding numbered item.

1.   ___ ___ ___ ___ ___ **H** ___ ___ ___ ___
2.   ___ ___ ___ **E** ___   ___ ___ ___ ___ ___
3. ___ ___ ___ ___ **A** ___ ___ ___ ___
4.   ___ ___ ___ ___ **L** ___ ___
5.   ___ ___ **T** ___
6.   ___ **H** ___ ___ ___ ___ ___ ___ ___ ___
7.   ___ ___ ___ ___ **Y** ___ ___ ___ ___ ___
8.   ___ ___ **D** ___ ___ ___
9.   ___ ___ **I** ___ ___ ___ ___
10.   ___ ___ ___ **E** ___ - ___ ___ ___ ___ ___ ___ ___
11.   ___ ___ ___ ___ **T** ___ ___ ___ ___ ___ ___

Clues

1. A mineral that is needed in a healthy diet to build strong teeth and bones.
2. A healthy diet includes only a few foods with this.
3. Nine of these are essential in a healthy diet.
4. The type of carbohydrate needed in a healthy diet.
5. Six to eight glasses of this are needed in a healthy diet.
6. A healthy diet helps reduce the amount of this in the bloodstream.
7. These chemicals from fat are essential in a healthy diet.
8. This mineral helps keep a good water balance in a healthy diet.
9. Food from these contain complete proteins.
10. Eat foods that contain these vitamins every day for a healthy diet.
11. The kind of fat to eat in a healthy diet.

CHAPTER 6 What Are Food Guides?   **Text Pages 36-45**

Study Guide

Completion: In the space to the left, write the word or words that **BEST** complete(s) each statement.

_____   1. Simple guidelines for making healthy food choices are called ___?___.

_____   2. Two commonly used food guides are ___?___ and ___?___.

_____

_____   3. Eating a variety of foods helps people get the ___?___ they need.

_____   4. ___?___ is the key to reaching and maintaining a healthy weight.

_____   5. ___?___ are used to measure the food energy your body needs.

_____   6. Weight stays the same when the calories ___?___ and ___?___ in a day are equal.

_____   7. Extra energy your body doesn't need is stored for future use as ___?___.

_____   8. Carbohydrates should make up ___?___% of a healthful diet.

_____   9. For a healthful diet, choose ___?___ fat.

_____   10. One gram of fat has ___?___ calories.

_____   11. Skim milk and lean meat are examples of ___?___ foods.

_____   12. The comparison of calories to nutrients is called ___?___.

_____   13. A type of food that usually has a(n) ___?___ nutrient density is sugary food.

_____   14. ___?___ is a medical problem linked to using too much sodium.

_____   15. Most sodium in the diet comes from ___?___

_____   16. The Pyramid suggests ___?___ servings of bread, cereal, rice, and pasta.

_____   17. Vegetables are generally good sources of vitamins ___?___ and ___?___.

_____

Continued on next page

_____ 18. The Food Guide Pyramid suggests ___?___ servings of fruits each day.

_____ 19. Eat ___?___ ounces of lean meat, poultry, or fish each day.

_____ 20. An important mineral from the Milk, Yogurt, and Cheese Group is ___?___.

Short Answer: Answer the following questions on the lines provided.

21. Who should use the Dietary Guidelines?

_____

22. Why is reaching and maintaining a healthy weight important? How can it be accomplished?

_____

_____

_____

23. What percent of a healthful diet should be carbohydrate? Fat? Protein?

_____

24. Why is a healthful diet low in fat, saturated fat, and cholesterol?

_____

25. Why should people eat plenty of vegetables, fruits, and grain products?

_____

_____

26. List three ways to cut down on the use of salt and sodium.

_____

_____

_____

27. How many servings are recommended for each food group in the Food Guide Pyramid?

_____

_____

_____

CHAPTER 6 **What Are Food Guides?** **Text Pages 36-45**

Food Groups and Nutrients

Directions: The five food groups from the Food Guide Pyramid are shown below. Match the nutrients listed below to the food groups from which they come. Write the letter of the food group(s) in the blank(s) to the left of each nutrient. Some nutrients are found in more than one food group, so blanks are given for each food group.

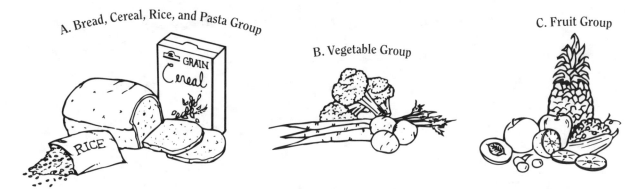

A. Bread, Cereal, Rice, and Pasta Group

B. Vegetable Group

C. Fruit Group

D. Meat, Poultry, Fish, Dry Beans, Eggs, and Nuts Group

E. Milk, Yogurt, and Cheese Group

Nutrients

1. ____ Calcium

2. ____ ____ ____ Carbohydrate

3. ____ ____ B vitamins

4. ____ ____ ____ Fiber

5. ____ ____ Iron

6. ____ Magnesium

7. ____ Potassium

8. ____ ____ Protein

9. ____ ____ Vitamin A

10. ____ ____ Vitamin C

11. ____ Zinc

Name _____ **Date** _____ **Class Hour** _____

CHAPTER 6 **What Are Food Guides?** **Text Pages 36-45**

   ## Hidden Foods

Directions: Hidden in the puzzle below are 20 common foods. They may be listed forwards, backwards, horizontally, or vertically. Circle the foods, then decide in which food group they belong in the Daily Food Guide. Write the name of the foods in the blanks under the correct food group names.

```
O  E  S  E  E  H  C  R  A  D  D  E  H  C  I
F  H  M  U  F  F  I  N  S  Y  E  K  R  U  T
R  A  P  P  L  E  R  F  P  Y  R  M  T  Y  G
G  M  S  L  A  E  M  T  A  O  A  K  O  L  R
I  B  P  E  N  J  K  I  R  V  R  L  R  I  A
L  U  L  T  B  T  P  E  A  R  E  I  T  N  P
O  R  I  T  A  T  R  U  G  O  Y  M  I  O  E
C  G  R  U  N  P  F  O  U  D  K  M  L  R  F
C  E  H  C  A  N  I  P  S  E  U  I  L  A  R
O  R  T  E  N  S  H  R  I  M  P  K  A  C  U
R  K  S  N  A  C  E  P  U  R  T  S  S  A  I
B  I  B  U  T  T  E  R  M  I  L  K  C  M  T
```

Bread, Cereal, Rice, and Pasta Group	Vegetable Group	Fruit Group	Meat, Poultry, Fish, Dry Beans, Eggs, and Nuts Group	Milk, Yogurt, and Cheese Group

34

Discovering Food and Nutrition Student Workbook Protected by Copyright ©

Study Guide

Completion: In the space to the left, write the word or words that **BEST** complete(s) each statement.

_____ 1. Your diet is affected by your ___?___, the patterns of your daily life.

_____ 2. A person who ___?___ good health might choose low-fat foods.

_____ 3. A person's ___?___ and ___?___ affect food likes and dislikes.

_____

_____ 4. New ___?___ and ___?___ give consumers more food choices.

_____

_____ 5. The main goal of food ___?___ is to sell food to consumers.

_____ 6. Comparing food and nutrition claims to what you already know can help you think ___?___ about them.

_____ 7. When evaluating food claims, consider how ___?___ and ___?___ the food is.

_____

_____ 8. There are ___?___ and ___?___ available that can evaluate your food choices.

_____

_____ 9. When choosing foods, the key terms to remember are ___?___ and ___?___.

_____

_____ 10. When and how many meals are eaten during a day are called a(n) ___?___.

_____ 11. Students who eat ___?___ have more interest in schoolwork and get better grades.

_____ 12. People on their own for meals should consider ___?___ and ___?___.

_____

_____ 13. Food needs change as people age and move through the ___?___.

Continued on next page

_____ 14. People who are ___?___ don't eat animal foods.

_____ 15. Athletes need lots of ___?___ for energy.

_____ 16. To replace perspiration lost during strenuous activity, athletes need lots of ___?___.

Short Answer: Answer the following questions on the lines provided.

17. What are three advantages of eating healthful foods?

_____

_____

_____

18. What are some common sources of information about food and nutrition? Do these sources provide accurate information?

_____

_____

19. Why doesn't it matter if your food choices aren't perfect each day?

_____

_____

_____

20. What are two common meal patterns?

_____

_____

21. What are two healthful options for lunches at school?

_____

_____

22. What are two low-fat options you could choose when eating out?

_____

_____

23. Will added protein, vitamins, and minerals help athletes perform better? Explain why or why not.

_____

_____

Name _____ **Date** _____ **Class Hour** _____

CHAPTER 7 Making Healthful Food Choices   **Text Pages 46-53**

"Souper" Salads

Diane and Carla went to the "Souper" Salads restaurant for lunch. Read the menu below and answer the questions on the lines provided.

"Souper" Salads Menu

—Salads—

Chef's Salad—assorted greens, strips of turkey and ham, sliced hard cooked eggs, cheese, and choice of dressing.

Fresh Fruit Salad—fresh fruit in season with yogurt dressing.

Spinach Salad—fresh spinach leaves, hard cooked eggs, grated Parmesan cheese, crisp bacon bits, and choice of dressing.

Pasta Salad—homemade pasta and fresh vegetables with herb dressing.

—Soups—

French Onion Soup
Cheese Soup
Chicken Noodle Soup

"Souper" Salad Combo— $4.99
soup, salad, and hot bread.

Soup or Salad— $2.99
Ala Cart

Beverages $1.00
Milk   Soft Drinks
Iced Tea   Coffee

1. Diane wants both soup and salad. Would it be less expensive to order the "Combo" or to order soup and salad ala carte. Explain.

_____

_____

2. Diane is trying to choose between the cheese soup and the chicken noodle soup. Which would be more healthful for her?

_____

_____

3. Carla decided to order the Spinach Salad. What would be her most healthful dressing choice?

_____

_____

4. Diane orders the "Combo" and water, while Carla ordered the Spinach Salad and milk. How much was their bill? How much change would they receive from a $10.00 bill?

_____

_____

CHAPTER 7 **Making Healthful Food Choices** **Text Pages 46-53**

   ## The Key to Food Choices

Directions: Complete this word scramble to identify one key to healthy food choices. The definition provides a clue for each word. Write the answer in the blanks provided, one letter per blank. Unscramble the circled letters to discover the word that belongs in the key.

1. __ __ __ __ __ ⃝ __ __ This is one influence on the food choices you make.

2. __ __ ⃝ __ __ __ __ __ __ __ __ This is used to sell food products.

3. __ __ __ __ __ __ __ __ __ __ __ ⃝ __ __ __ What is needed to evaluate food information.

4. __ __ __ __ __ __ ⃝ __ __ __ A term that means avoiding extremes when making food choices.

5. __ __ __ __ __ __ __ __ __ ⃝ __ __ When snacks and meals are eaten during the day.

6. __ __ ⃝ __ __ __ These are part of a total eating plan for each day.

7. __ __ __ __ __ __ __ __ __ __ ⃝ __ __ __ Athletes need more of this nutrient than other people do.

8. __ __ __ __ __ __ __

Discovering Food and Nutrition Student Workbook Protected by Copyright ©

Study Guide

Completion: In the space at the left, write the word or words that **BEST** complete(s) each statement.

_____ 1. Using ___?___ skills when shopping helps get the best nutrition and quality.

_____ 2. The weather and the time of year affect the ___?___ of food.

_____ 3. A great variety of foods are found in stores called ___?___.

_____ 4. Food is often displayed in cardboard boxes in ___?___ stores.

_____ 5. Small shops where foods are usually more expensive are ___?___ stores.

_____ 6. Food shoppers who are ___?___ may buy more than they need.

_____ 7. The steps taken to prepare and package food for sale are called ___?___.

_____ 8. ___?___ or ___?___ foods have added nutrients.

_____

_____ 9. ___?___ foods have been processed to make them easier to store or use.

_____ 10. Highly-processed foods usually contain fewer ___?___ than less-processed ones.

_____ 11. Make your shopping ___?___ based on your plans for upcoming meals and snacks.

_____ 12. Basic foods (such as flour) that are always kept on hand are called ___?___.

_____ 13. Grocery items stored in large bins are called ___?___ foods.

_____ 14. Fruits and vegetables are found in the ___?___ department of the super-market.

_____ 15. Find most economical brand and size package by using ___?___.

_____ 16. Open dating helps you know whether food is ___?___.

_____ 17. The way a food is handled and stored affects its ___?___.

_____ 18. The weight of the food is called the ___?___ weight.

Continued on next page

_____ 19. The ingredient list on a label is based on ___?___.

_____ 20. Computer checkout systems are based on the ___?___.

_____ 21. Buying a product because it appeals at the moment is called ___?___.

Short Answer: Answer the following questions on the lines provided.

22. What should you consider if you decide to shop at more than one food store?

_____

_____

23. What factors should you consider in deciding how often to buy food?

_____

24. Why is planning meals the first step in making a shopping list?

_____

_____

_____

25. Identify at least four categories that can be used to group foods on a shopping list.

_____

_____

_____

26. What is the benefit of unit pricing? How can you use it when you shop?

_____

_____

27. On what items can you expect to see open dating?

_____

28. What kind of nutritional information is found on food labels?

_____

_____

29. What are three kinds of information to compare to get the best values when shopping for food?

_____

_____

CHAPTER 8 Shopping for Food   **Text Pages 54-61**

Unit Pricing

Directions: Read the situations described below. Calculate the unit price of each product. Then tell which product you would recommend buying and explain why.

Rona is buying oatmeal. She serves it several days a week for breakfast and makes oatmeal cookies often. The grocery store has 18 oz. (510 g) for $1.72 and 42 oz. (1.19 kg) for $2.98. Which should Rona buy?

1. Unit price:

   18 oz. (510 g) _____   42 oz (1.19 kg) _____

2. Recommendations: _____

   _____

3. Explanation: _____

   _____

Sergio is buying potatoes for his family. He finds a 5 lb. (2.3 kg) sack of potatoes for $1.99 and a 20 lb. (9 kg) sack for $4.99. Sergio has plenty of room to store the larger sack, but his family doesn't eat many potatoes. Which should Sergio buy?

4. Unit price:

   5 lb. (2.3 kg) sack_____   20 lb. (9 kg) sack_____

5. Recommendations: _____

   _____

6. Explanation: _____

   _____

Meredith is buying long grain rice. The 10 oz. (280 g) package costs $0.49. A large 10 lb. (5 kg) package costs $4.99. Meredith uses enough rice to buy the large package, but doesn't have space in her kitchen to store it.

7. Unit price:

   10 oz. (280 g) package_____   10 lb. (5 kg) package_____

8. Recommendations: _____

   _____

9. Explanation: _____

   _____

Name _____ **Date** _____ **Class Hour** _____

CHAPTER **8** Shopping for Food   **Text Pages 54-61**

 Grocery Shopping

Directions: Listed below are clues that have to do with grocery shopping. Use each clue to fill in the blanks in the corresponding numbered item. The letters in the darker squares will spell a term that is a tool to use in buying food.

1.
2.
3.
4.
5.
6.
7.
8.
9.
10.

Clues

1. These depend on weather, time of year, packaging, and transportation.

2. Put raw meat and poultry in this kind of bag.

3. How food should be handled in the supermarket.

4. This allows you to compare costs.

5. If you make these wisely, you will get the most for your money.

6. These provide valuable information.

7. Some foods lose this if not brought home and stored immediately.

8. A kind of food buying to avoid.

9. This is often the least expensive brand.

10. Avoid this kind of container when buying food.

Study Guide

Completion: In the space to the left, write the word or words that **BEST** answer(s) each question.

_____ 1. What kind of appliances are the range and refrigerator?

_____ 2. What are appliances called that can be used wherever there is an electric outlet?

_____ 3. What is an appliance that provides heat for cooking food?

_____ 4. In what kind of oven does hot air circulate around the pan?

_____ 5. Where does food cook first when being baked in a conventional oven?

_____ 6. Where is the heating unit located in the broiler?

_____ 7. What kind of oven contains fans that circulate hot air at high speeds?

_____ 8. What is an oven called that cooks with tiny waves of energy?

_____ 9. In comparing ovens, which type uses the least energy?

_____ 10. What is the maximum cooking power range in microwave ovens?

_____ 11. What are the two basic types of refrigerators?

_____ 12. How full should a refrigerator be for best efficiency?

_____ 13. What should be used with warm water to clean the inside of a refrigerator-freezer?

_____ 14. What is a small appliance that cooks food slowly at low temperatures?

_____ 15. What is a small appliance that cuts, chops, minces, blends, and liquifies food?

_____ 16. What is a small appliance that can be used for chopping, slicing, mixing ingredients, and kneading dough?

_____ 17. How is an appliance labeled if it can be put in water?

_____ 18. What label shows that appliances have been tested for safety?

Continued on next page

Short Answer: Answer the following questions on the lines provided.

19. Compare a cooking time in conventional, convection, and microwave ovens.

_____

_____

_____

20. Why should you adjust the oven racks before turning on heat?

_____

_____

_____

21. Describe how food is cooked in the microwave oven.

_____

_____

_____

22. How should the freezer section in a one-door refrigerator be used? Why?

_____

_____

_____

23. Why should the shelves of a refrigerator or freezer be left uncovered?

_____

_____

24. What happens when frost builds up in the freezer? What can be done about it?

_____

_____

_____

25. What are the main advantages of using small appliances?

_____

_____

CHAPTER 9 Using Kitchen Appliances   **Text Pages 62-67**

Identifying Small Appliances

Directions: Several small appliances are pictured below. The names of these appliances are given in scrambled form. Unscramble each word and write it in the blank above the appliance it names.

xrmei   tcieeclr tleksil   rasttoe   aosrett vnoe

wlos orckoe   dofo sropscroe   dreenlb

1. _____

2. _____

3. _____

4. _____

5. _____

6. _____

7. _____

CHAPTER 9 Using Kitchen Appliances **Text Pages 62-67**

What Are the Consequences?

Directions: Read the situations described below. Then answer each item as directed.

1. Raul stood in front of the refrigerator trying to decide what to have for lunch. Because he couldn't decide, he shut the refrigerator door and opened the freezer door to see what was in there. What are the consequences of his actions?

_____

_____

2. Cheri is warming soup in a large pan for lunch. She turned on the small front burner of the range to heat the soup. What are the consequences of her actions?

_____

_____

3. Shane wanted to check on the casserole he had cooking in the oven, so he leaned his face down toward the oven door and opened it a crack to peek at the casserole. What could be the consequences of his actions?

_____

_____

4. Janice bought some fresh English muffins. When she got home, she decided to freeze them for later use, so she put them in the freezing compartment of her one-door refrigerator. What are the probable consequences of her action?

_____

_____

5. When Shireen took the last pork chop out of the electric skillet, she unplugged the skillet and turned it off. What could have been the consequences of her actions?

_____

_____

Study Guide

Completion: In the space to the left, write the word or words that **BEST** complete(s) each statement.

_____   1. Using ___?___ and ___?___ will help prevent burns from hot pans.

_____

_____   2. There are at least ___?___ different cups in a measuring set.

_____   3. A measuring cup with an extra space at the top is for measuring ___?___.

_____   4. A(n) ___?___ knife is the most likely to cause an accident.

_____   5. Protect the countertop or table while cutting foods by using a(n) ___?___.

_____   6. A tool that grates food into tiny pieces is a(n) ___?___.

_____   7. A tool that removes peel from fruits and vegetables is a(n) ___?___.

_____   8. An all-purpose knife is also called a(n) ___?___ knife.

_____   9. A knife with a sawtooth edge is a(n) ___?___ knife.

_____   10. A tool that adds air to dry ingredients is a(n) ___?___.

_____   11. A wire ___?___ is often used to beat egg white mixtures.

_____   12. A tool for light beating is a(n) ___?___ beater.

_____   13. A tool used to cut shortening into flour is a(n) ___?___.

_____   14. A tool used to remove food from spoons, bowls, and jars is a(n) ___?___.

_____   15. Use a(n) ___?___ to level off dry or solid ingredients when measuring.

_____   16. To drain liquid from food, use a(n) ___?___ spoon.

_____   17. ___?___ let the cook lift and turn hot food without piercing it.

_____   18. A tool used to dip liquid from one container to another is a(n) ___?___.

_____   19. A tool for rolling out dough for pie crust is a(n) ___?___.

Continued on next page

_____ 20. Use a(n) ___?___ to hold hot food while it cools.

_____ 21. A ___?___ is used to drain liquid from foods.

_____ 22. A pan with one long handle is a(n) ___?___.

_____ 23. A(n) ___?___ holds food above boiling water in a pot or pan.

_____ 24. A shallow pan with handles on both ends and a rack is a(n) ___?___.

Short Answer: Answer the following questions on the lines provided.

25. Why should coffee cups and spoons used on the table not be used for measuring ingredients for cooking?

_____

_____

_____

26. Why should a liquid measuring cup be used for measuring liquids?

_____

27. Name four kinds of knives and tell what cutting jobs each does best.

_____

_____

_____

28. What kind of tools should be used with pans with a nonstick finish? Why?

_____

_____

_____

_____

29. List the various materials from which cookware can be made. Where can each be used?

_____

_____

30. Why do baking pans come in a wide variety of shapes and sizes? Give examples.

_____

_____

_____

CHAPTER 10 **Know Your Equipment**   **Text Pages 68-73**

   Identifying Equipment

Directions: Match each equipment name below with the correct sketch of the equipment. Write the letter of the equipment name in the blank above each pictured item. Do not use any name more than once. Some names will not be used.

A. Chef's knife
D. Dry measuring cups
G. Ladle
J. Peeler
M. Rubber scraper
P. Spatula

B. Colander
E. Grater
H. Liquid measuring cup
K. Rolling pin
N. Serrated knife
Q. Tongs

C. Cutting board
F. Kitchen shears
I. Pastry blender
L. Rotary beater
O. Sifter
R. Wire cooling rack

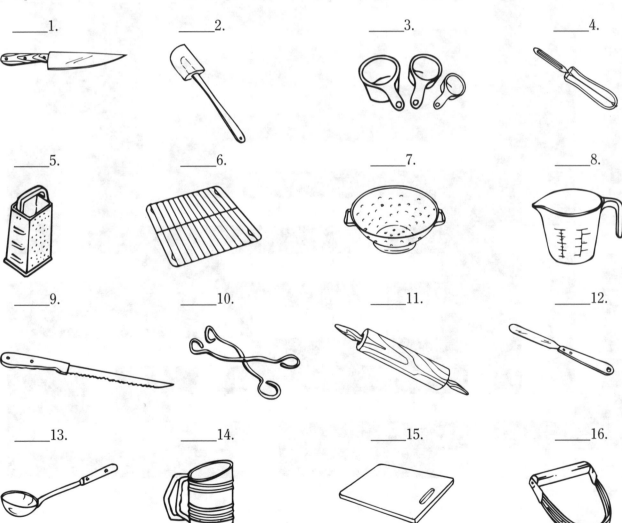

_____1.   _____2.   _____3.   _____4.

_____5.   _____6.   _____7.   _____8.

_____9.   _____10.   _____11.   _____12.

_____13.   _____14.   _____15.   _____16.

Equipment Crossword

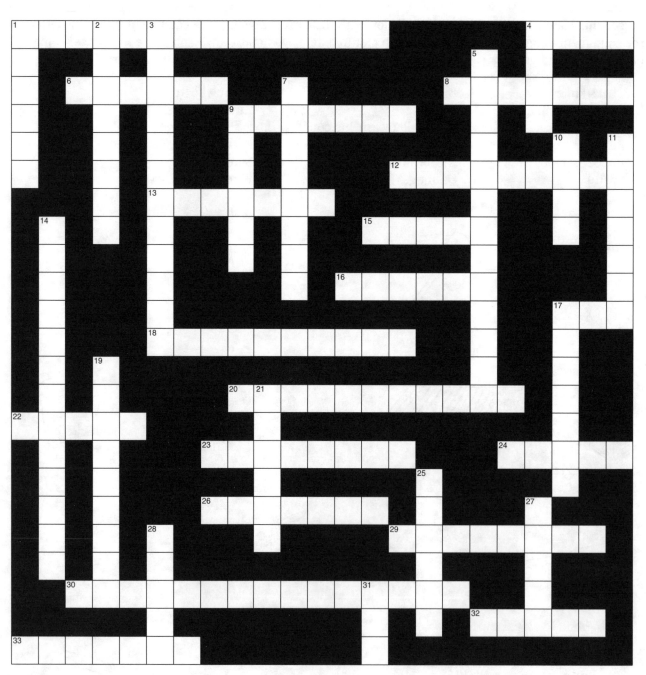

Continued on next page

CHAPTER 10 Know Your Equipment   **Text Pages 68-73**

Equipment Crossword

Directions: Fill in the crossword puzzle by placing the answer to each clue in the appropriate space.

Across

1. Use this to measure baking powder for biscuits. (2 words)
4. Cut this with a slicing knife.
6. Use this tool to grate carrots for salad.
8. Use this board to protect the counter from nicks and cuts.
9. This spoon will help you lift cooked vegetables from their cooking liquid.
12. This tool is used to beat and blend. (2 words)
13. This spoon has a long heatproof handle.
15. Use these to turn chicken without piercing it.
16. Use this tool to remove the skins from potatoes.
17. A cooking container with two small handles.
18. Use this to roll out biscuit dough. (2 words)
20. A useful tool to lift or turn food. (2 words)
22. Material often used to make casserole dishes.
23. Use this tool to cool rolls or bread. (2 words)
24. This protects clothing from spots or stains.
26. This can be used in cooking vegetables to hold the food above boiling water.
29. Another name for cooking and baking pans.
30. Use to discover whether a turkey is done roasting. (2 words)
32. Use this knife to chop broccoli.
33. Loosen a loaf of banana bread from the pan with this tool.

Down

1. These bowls are usually made of pottery, glass, or metal.
2. Use this knife to cut a loaf of bread.
3. Use this tool to mix pancake batter. (2 words)
4. Use this to protect yourself when removing food from the oven.
5. Use this to remove the last bit of peanut butter from the jar. (2 words)
7. Drain the water from noodles with this.
9. This tool will remove lumps from flour.
10. Use a liquid measuring cup to measure this.
11. This piece of cookware commonly comes in 10- and 12-inch (25- and 30-cm) sizes.
14. Use this tool to cut the fat into flour when making biscuits. (2 words)
17. This kind of pot is only for oven use.
19. Use this type of cookware to bake a macaroni-ground beef dish.
21. This tool is useful in turning over hamburgers during cooking.
25. The kind of spoon used to mix and stir.
27. Use this to put soup into serving bowls.
28. Cooking utensils made from this material can be used either on the range or in the oven.
31. A rotary beater can be used to beat this.

CHAPTER 10 Know Your Equipment   **Text Pages 68-73**

What Equipment Is Needed?

Directions: Read the situations described below. List the equipment needed on the lines provided.

1. Francessca is making a loaf of applesauce bread. The recipe includes sifted flour, milk, baking soda, applesauce, a beaten egg, and spices. What equipment does Francessca need to make and bake this recipe?

   _____

   _____

   _____

   _____

2. David is making a tossed salad for supper. He's using lettuce, grated carrots, sliced celery and cucumbers, green olives, and kidney beans. What equipment does he need to make this salad?

   _____

   _____

   _____

   _____

3. Kaitlin is making sauce to serve over spaghetti. The sauce recipe takes ground beef, chopped onions and green peppers, sliced celery, tomato sauce, and several spices. What equipment will Kaitlin need to make the spaghetti and sauce?

   _____

   _____

   _____

   _____

CHAPTER 11 **Reading Recipes**   **Text Pages 74-81**

Study Guide

Completion: In the space to the left, write the word or words that **BEST** complete(s) each statement.

_____ 1. The foods in a recipe are called ___?___.

_____ 2. The directions of a recipe should give clear ___?___ instructions.

_____ 3. The amount a recipe makes or the number of servings is the ___?___.

_____ 4. ___?___ are made from recipes that should be followed exactly.

_____ 5. You should use a(n) ___?___ and a(n) ___?___ when cutting foods.

_____ 6. To remove a thin layer of peel from a fruit or vegetable is to ___?___ it.

_____ 7. To ___?___ a food is to cut it into thin, flat pieces.

_____ 8. Food that is cut in small irregular pieces is called ___?___.

_____ 9. Food that is chopped into pieces as small as possible is called ___?___.

_____ 10. One way to shred food is to rub it on the large holes of a ___?___.

_____ 11. To ___?___ food use a food mill or blender to make a smooth, thick mass.

_____ 12. The two motions used to stir food are ___?___ and ___?___.

_____
_____ 13. Two terms that mean to stir ingredients together are ___?___ and ___?___.

_____
_____ 14. To mix ingredients until they are uniform use a ___?___, ___?___, or ___?___.
_____
_____

_____ 15. Combining shortening and sugar is called ___?___.

_____ 16. When ingredients are ___?___, they are beaten rapidly to increase volume.

_____ 17. A gentle way to combine two mixtures is to ___?___.

_____ 18. To ___?___ is a way to mix shortening and flour.

_____ 19. ___?___ an oven to get it to the right temperature before you put in the food.

Continued on next page

_____ 20. A liquid that is not quite hot enough to boil is ___?___.

_____ 21. To ___?___ means to brush or pour liquid over a food as it cooks.

Short Answer: Answer the following questions on the lines provided.

22. What basic information should a recipe provide so it can be made successfully?

_____

_____

23. What are the similarities and differences between cubing and dicing?

_____

_____

_____

24. What is the difference between stirring and beating a mixture?

_____

_____

_____

_____

_____

25. Explain how to fold in ingredients.

_____

_____

_____

26. Explain the different ways food can be browned. How do you know which method to choose?

_____

_____

_____

27. What does it mean to drain food? What equipment can be used?

_____

_____

_____

28. What is the purpose of a garnish?

_____

CHAPTER 11 Reading Recipes   **Text Pages 74-81**

Understanding the Recipe

Directions: Read the recipe and answer the questions below on the lines provided.

Quick Beef Pie

Customary		Ingredients	Metric	Directions
1	lb.	Ground Beef	500 g	
1		Onion, chopped	1	1. **Preheat** oven to 350°F (180°C).
10¾	oz. can	Condensed tomato soup	305 g can	2. **Crumble** ground beef in skillet. Add onion and cook until browned.
16	oz. can	Green beans, drained	500 g can	3. **Spoon** off excess fat.
¼	tsp.	Ground pepper	1 mL	4. **Add** tomato soup, green beans, and pepper.
1½	cup	Mashed potatoes	375 mL	5. **Simmer** five minutes.
⅓	cup	Shredded cheddar cheese	75 mL	6. **Grease** casserole dish. Pour meat mixture into casserole.

Yield: 4 servings

Pan: 12-inch (31 cm) skillet
2-quart (2 L) casserole dish

7. **Drop** potatoes in mounds onto hot meat mixture.
8. **Sprinkle** with shredded cheese.
9. **Bake** for 20 minutes.

1. What ingredients are used to make this recipe?

_____

2. What size measuring cups and spoons are needed to make this recipe? _____

_____

3. What tools are needed to chop the onion? _____

4. What will the onion be like after it is chopped? _____

_____

5. What does it mean to drain the green beans? What tool(s) could be used to drain them?

_____

6. What tool would you use to shred the cheese? _____

7. What is the yield of this recipe? _____

CHAPTER 11 Reading Recipes   **Text Pages 74-81**

   Magic Terms Square

Directions: Find the term that best fits each description. Write the number of the correct term in the space in the lettered square. If all your answers are correct, the total of the numbers, or the "Magic Number," will be the same in each row across and down. Write the Magic Number in the space provided.

Terms

1. baste	11. mince		
2. beat	12. pare		
3. boil	13. preheat		
4. chill	14. puree		
5. cream	15. shred		
6. cube	16. slice		
7. cut in	17. stir		
8. drain	18. toss		
9. fold in	19. whip		
10. garnish			

A	B	C	D
E	F	G	H
I	J	K	L
M	N	O	P

The Magic Number is _____.

Descriptions

A. To mix with a rotary beater or electric mixer.
B. To mix shortening and flour with a pastry blender.
C. To tumble a mixture very lightly with a spoon and fork.
D. To cut a thin layer of peel from fruits or vegetables.
E. To remove excess liquid from a food.
F. To combine shortening and sugar until soft and smooth.
G. To chop food until the pieces are as small as possible.
H. To cut food into long, thin pieces.
I. To turn on an oven ahead of time.
J. To mix using a circular or figure eight motion.
K. To cut into pieces that are the same size.
L. To heat a liquid until bubbles constantly rise to the surface and break.
M. To cut into thin, flat pieces.
N. To decorate a food or dish with a small, colorful food.
O. To refrigerate food until it is cold.
P. To gently combine two mixtures.

CHAPTER 12 Recipe Math    **Text Pages 82-87**

Study Guide

Completion: In the space to the left, write the word or words that **BEST** complete(s) each statement.

_____   1. Two systems of measurement are the ___?___ system and the ___?___ system.

_____   2. The system of measurement which is most commonly used in the United States is the ___?___.

_____   3. The measuring system used in most of the world is the ___?___.

_____   4. Two measurements that are the same as each other are called ___?___.

_____   5. How ___?___ or ___?___ an ingredient is is called weight.

_____   6. The tool used to measure weight is a(n) ___?___.

_____   7. The two basic units of weight in the customary system are the ___?___ and the ___?___.

_____   8. The basic unit of weight in the metric system is the ___?___.

_____   9. The customary equivalent of one pound is ___?___ ounces.

_____   10. The space an ingredient takes up is called ___?___.

_____   11. To measure the space an ingredient takes up requires ___?___.

_____   12. A(n) ___?___ is used to measure both weight and volume.

_____   13. The customary equivalent of 1 tablespoon is ___?___ teaspoon(s).

_____   14. The customary equivalent of 1 fluid ounce is ___?___ tablespoon(s).

_____   15. It takes 16 tablespoons to make ___?___ cup(s).

_____   16. The customary equivalent of 1 quart is ___?___ ounces.

Continued on next page

_____ 17. In metric measures, temperature is measured in ___?___.

_____ 18. Millimeters or centimeters are measures of ___?___ in the metric system.

_____ 19. By increasing or decreasing a recipe, you can change the ___?___.

_____ 20. If the recipe says it makes 4 servings and you want to serve 12, you would multiply the ingredient amounts by ___?___.

_____ 21. When you have decreased a recipe, cook the food in a ___?___ pan.

Short Answer: Answer the following questions on the lines provided.

22. Why is it usually not necessary to convert measurements from one system to another?

_____

_____

_____

23. Explain the relationship between cups, pints, quarts, and gallons.

_____

_____

_____

24. What is the difference between yield and desired yield?

_____

_____

25. What is the formula for increasing or decreasing a recipe?

_____

_____

26. When increasing or decreasing a recipe, why should the cook figure out the new amounts and write them down before starting?

_____

_____

_____

27. Explain how rounding off ingredient measurements would affect a stew and a cake. Why?

_____

_____

Measuring Match Ups

Directions: Match each measuring term in the left column with the correct abbreviation from the right column. Write the letter of the abbreviation in the space provided. Do not use any abbreviation more than once. Some abbreviations will not be used.

Measuring Terms	**Abbreviations**
____ 1. Celsius	A. kg
____ 2. Centimeter	B. m
____ 3. Cup	C. pd.
____ 4. Gallon	D. lb.
____ 5. Gram	E. C
____ 6. Inch	F. L
____ 7. Kilogram	G. oz.
____ 8. Liter	H. g
____ 9. Milliliter	I. tsp.
____ 10. Millimeter	J. qt.
____ 11. Ounce	K. cm
____ 12. Pint	L. pt.
____ 13. Pound	M. Tbsp.
____ 14. Quart	N. c.
____ 15. Tablespoon	O. gal.
____ 16. Teaspoon	P. mL
	Q. in.
	R. mm

Hidden Measurements

Directions: Eighteen measuring terms are hidden in the puzzle below. Circle the terms, which may appear forward, backward, horizontally, or vertically. As you discover the terms, write them in the chart on the next page. When you have found all the terms, complete the chart with the term's abbreviation, whether it is used in the customary or metric system, and what the term measures (volume, length, etc.)

```
G  O  S  E  C  N  U  O  D  I  U  L  F
A  M  T  N  A  L  O  U  N  C  E  G  A
L  I  R  S  S  M  A  B  U  L  R  Q  H
L  H  A  T  R  V  O  K  O  W  E  U  R
O  P  U  C  E  B  Y  I  P  P  T  J  E
N  K  Q  D  T  M  G  L  C  R  I  T  N
T  A  B  L  E  S  P  O  O  N  L  E  H
H  C  N  I  M  F  I  G  O  K  I  A  E
Y  O  L  P  I  N  T  R  Z  A  L  S  I
E  M  I  M  T  C  E  A  P  R  L  P  T
H  A  T  O  N  X  B  M  D  W  I  O  U
S  R  E  T  E  M  I  L  L  I  M  O  Q
S  G  R  C  C  E  L  S  I  U  S  N  E
```

Continued on next page

CHAPTER 12 Recipe Math   **Text Pages 82-87**

   Hidden Measurements

Term	Abbreviation	Customary or Metric	What it Measures
1.			
2.			
3.			
4.			
5.			
6.			
7.			
8.			
9.			
10.			
11.			
12.			
13.			
14.			
15.			
16.			
17.			
18.			

Looking at Equivalents

Directions: Look at the two measurement terms listed in the lenses of the glasses below and write the equivalent measure in the space provided.

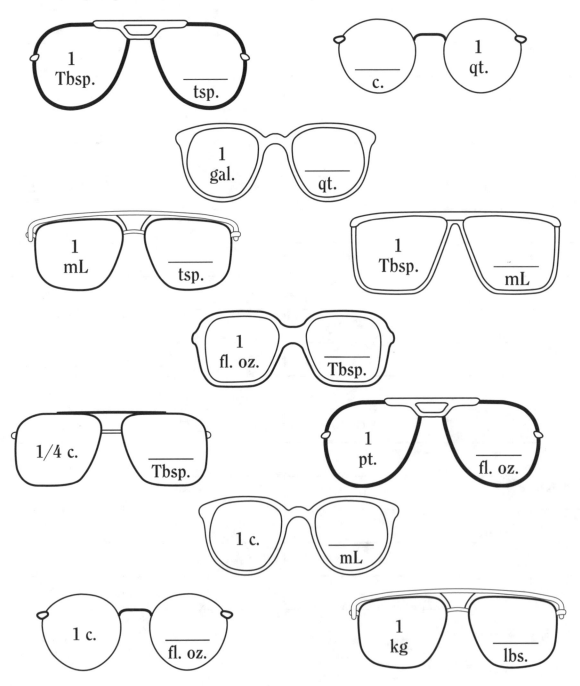

1 Tbsp. = _____ tsp.

_____ c. = 1 qt.

1 gal. = _____ qt.

1 mL = _____ tsp.

1 Tbsp. = _____ mL

1 fl. oz. = _____ Tbsp.

1/4 c. = _____ Tbsp.

1 pt. = _____ fl. oz.

1 c. = _____ mL

1 c. = _____ fl. oz.

1 kg = _____ lbs.

Study Guide

Completion: In the space to the left, write the word or words that **BEST** complete(s) each statement.

_____ 1. Dry ingredients should be ___?___ with the top of the measuring cup.

_____ 2. Small amounts of ingredients are measured with measuring ___?___.

_____ 3. At first, fill the measuring cup or spoon so that it ___?___ slightly.

_____ 4. Level off the dry ingredients with a spatula or another ___?___ edge.

_____ 5. A dry ingredient with its particles separated has been ___?___.

_____ 6. Flours that should not be sifted are ___?___, such as whole wheat or rye.

_____ 7. Whole wheat flour should be ___?___ with a spoon before measuring.

_____ 8. In measuring brown sugar, ___?___ the sugar into the cup with the back of a spoon.

_____ 9. If granulated or powdered sugar is ___?___ it should be strained.

_____ 10. Milk or water should be measured in a ___?___ measuring cup.

_____ 11. Have the liquid measuring cup on a ___?___ surface when measuring.

_____ 12. The measurement of liquid should be checked at ___?___.

_____ 13. To measure honey or syrup ___?___ the measuring cup.

_____ 14. To remove honey or syrup from a measuring cup use a(n) ___?___.

_____ 15. Use measuring ___?___ to measure small amounts of liquid.

_____ 16. To measure solid fats use the ___?___ or ___?___ method.

_____ 17. One stick of butter or margarine equals ___?___ cup (mL).

_____ 18. To get air bubbles out, ___?___ shortening into the cup.

_____ 19. Use a ___?___ to get shortening out of a dry measuring cup.

Continued on next page

Short Answer: Answer the following questions on the lines provided.

20. Why is measuring ingredients accurately important in preparing food?

_____

21. What are three "don'ts" when filling a measuring cup with dry ingredients?

_____

_____

_____

22. What is the difference between measuring brown sugar and flour?

_____

_____

_____

23. Describe how to check the level of liquid in a measuring cup. Why is this necessary?

_____

_____

_____

24. Why should you hold the measuring spoon away from the mixing bowl when measuring liquids?

_____

_____

_____

25. How can you use the stick method of measuring butter or margarine if you need 2 tablespoons? What is the advantage of using this method?

_____

_____

_____

26. How do you sift flour? Why do you do it? What does it do to the flour?

_____

_____

CHAPTER 13 Basic Measuring Methods   **Text Pages 88-91**

Choosing Measuring Methods

Directions: The ingredients shown below are measured with a variety of measuring methods. Match each ingredient with two or more of the measuring methods listed below. Write the letter of the appropriate measuring methods in the blanks under the ingredients. There is one blank for each measuring method.

1. ___ ___ ___   2. ___ ___ ___   3. ___ ___ ___   4. ___ ___ ___

5. ___ ___ ___   6. ___ ___ ___   7. ___ ___ ___   8. ___ ___ ___

Measuring Methods

A. Use a dry measuring cup.
B. Use a liquid measuring cup.
C. May need sifting (or straining) before use.
D. Check measurement at eye level.
E. Pack firmly in cup.
F. Level with a straight edge.
G. Never sift.
H. Be sure to work out air bubbles.
I. Measure on a flat surface.
J. Grease or oil cup before measuring.

CHAPTER 13 Basic Measuring Methods

Recipe Measuring

Directions: Given below is the ingredient list for a recipe of Butterscotch Bars. On the lines below, explain what type and size of cups or spoons should be used and how the listed ingredient should be measured.

Butterscotch Bars

Customary	Ingredients	Metric
½ cup	Butter or margarine	125 mL
1½ cups	Brown sugar	375 mL
2	Eggs	2
1 tsp.	Vanilla	5 mL
1½ cups	Sifted flour	375 mL
2 tsp.	Baking powder	10 mL

1. Butter or margarine:

   _____

   _____

2. Brown sugar:

   _____

   _____

3. Vanilla:

   _____

   _____

4. Sifted flour:

   _____

   _____

5. Baking powder:

   _____

   _____

CHAPTER 14 Basic Cooking Methods   **Text Pages 92-99**

Study Guide

Completion: In the space to the left, write the word or words that **BEST** complete(s) each statement.

_____ 1. Baking, broiling, and roasting use the ___?___ method.

_____ 2. When foods are cooked in dry heat, they usually turn ___?___.

_____ 3. ___?___ uses direct heat from above.

_____ 4. The oven door is usually ___?___ when broiling in an electric oven.

_____ 5. A method of broiling food on the rangetop is ___?___.

_____ 6. Two methods of cooking food in dry heat in an oven are ___?___ and
_____   ___?___.

_____ 7. The ___?___ method uses steam, hot liquid, or a combination.

_____ 8. ___?___ the pan to keep moisture and steam inside.

_____ 9. When a food ___?___, bubbles rise slowly but do not break the surface.

_____ 10. A ___?___ holds food above boiling water, but lets the steam flow
                            through.

_____ 11. Cooking in fat is called ___?___.

_____ 12. When frying food, the ___?___method adds the most fat to the food.

_____ 13. Panfrying foods like vegetables to precook them is known as ___?___.

_____ 14. Hot fat may spatter when frying if the food to be fried is ___?___.

_____ 15. To ___?___, brown food in fat and cook slowly in moist heat.

_____ 16. A high temperature and a small amount of oil are used to cook food
                            quickly when using the ___?___ method.

_____ 17. ___?___ can be destroyed by heat, causing food to be less healthful.

_____ 18. More nutrients are lost when food is cut in ___?___ pieces.

Continued on next page

_____ 19. Protein foods should be cooked at ___?___ temperatures.

_____ 20. Cooking liquids that contain ___?___ should be served with the food or saved for another use.

Short Answer: Answer the following questions on the lines provided.

21. Name the two parts of a broiler pan and explain the purpose of each.

_____

_____

_____

22. How do you control how fast food cooks when it is broiled?

_____

_____

23. Describe how to panbroil a hamburger.

_____

_____

_____

24. Is the microwave considered a dry heat method? Why or why not?

_____

_____

25. Why are other cooking methods more healthful than frying?

_____

_____

26. Explain the main difference between deep-fat frying and panfrying.

_____

_____

_____

27. Identify three ways that nutrients can be lost when food is prepared.

_____

_____

_____

Name _____ Date _____ Class Hour_____

CHAPTER **14** Basic Cooking Methods

Text Pages 92-99

   Hidden Cooking Terms

Directions: Hidden in the puzzle below are 13 cooking terms. The terms may appear forward, backward, horizontally, or vertically. Circle each term in the puzzle. Decide which type of cooking method each term is and write it in the appropriate space in the chart below.

```
G N I Y R F H C N E R F S
N R B H C G L R F S T M M
I N S O G N I S I A R B B
V T T R B I W B S B P I R
A Y E V O Y D O E A A N O
W P A N B R O I L I N G I
O G M N S F D L I N F N L
R N I G J R E I K F R I I
C I N G I I P N Z F Y E N
I K G O T T O G S M I T G
M A R O A S T I N G N U I
A B A I N G A I C N G A S
G E T G N I R E M M I S P
```

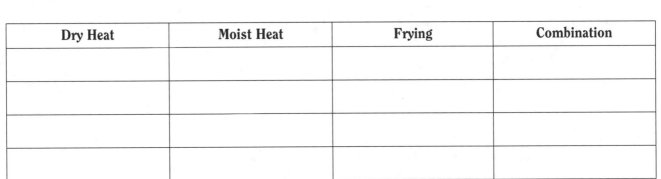

Dry Heat	Moist Heat	Frying	Combination

CHAPTER 14 Basic Cooking Methods **Text Pages 92-99**

▼ ▼ ▼ Actions and Consequences

Directions: Given below are situations involving foods and different cooking methods. Read each item and explain what will be the consequences of the action(s) taken.

1. Janine is panbroiling ground beef patties in a skillet. The grease is spattering on the range, the counter, and her clothes, so she puts a cover on the skillet. What will be the consequences of her action?

   _____

   _____

2. Asif is broiling chicken for dinner. He doesn't like to wash the broiler pan so he lines the grid with aluminum foil. What will be the consequences of his action?

   _____

   _____

3. Kelley is broiling a steak. Because it is thick and she wants it well done, she puts it close to the heating element. What will be the consequences of her action?

   _____

   _____

4. Dylan is simmering potatoes for potato salad. He is in a hurry, so he turns up the heat until the potatoes are boiling vigorously. What will be the consequences of his action?

   _____

   _____

5. Luisa is steaming broccoli. She puts the steamer basket in the pan, but doesn't cover the pan as the broccoli cooks. What will be the consequences of her action?

   _____

   _____

6. Ginny is making scrambled eggs for breakfast. She melts the butter in a small skillet over high heat and then adds the eggs to cook. What will be the consequences of her action?

   _____

   _____

Study Guide

Completion: In the space to the left, write the word or words that **BEST** complete(s) each statement.

_____ 1. One advantage of microwave cooking is that it saves preparation ___?___.

_____ 2. Use the ___?___ setting on the microwave to thaw frozen foods.

_____ 3. Microwave ovens create heat through ___?___.

_____ 4. Microwaves are tiny waves of ___?___.

_____ 5. The ___?___ of a microwave oven is the amount of electricity used to create microwaves.

_____ 6. The microwave oven with the most ___?___ cooks food fastest.

_____ 7. The ___?___ on the microwave controls the amount of cooking power.

_____ 8. Materials such as glass and paper allow microwaves to ___?___ them.

_____ 9. Paper and plastics that do not say "microwave-safe" could cause a ___?___.

_____ 10. Casseroles and liquid measuring cups made of heatproof ___?___ are safe.

_____ 11. Microwaves can cause ___?___ and damage the oven if metal cookware is used.

_____ 12. In ___?___, ___?___, or ___?___ pans, microwaves get to the food from all angles.

_____

_____

_____ 13. Food in the corners of a square pan will ___?___ in the microwave.

_____ 14. When microwaving several individual items, arrange them in a ___?___ pattern.

_____ 15. Cover cookware with ___?___ wrap if you want to hold moisture in the dish.

_____ 16. Foods that are ___?___ in the microwave are hard, tough, and dry.

Continued on next page

_____ 17. ___?___ is a period when the food continues to cook after microwaving.

_____ 18. ___?___ batches of food are easier to cook and handle in the microwave.

_____ 19. Remove the cover after microwaving so the ___?___ flows away from the face.

_____ 20. Pierce ___?___ before microwaving or they may explode in the oven.

Short Answer: Answer the following questions on the lines provided.

21. Explain how to tell whether or not cookware is safe to use in the microwave?

_____

_____

_____

22. When food is not uniform in size and shape, how should it be arranged for microwaving?

_____

_____

23. Why should brown paper bags or products made from recycled paper not be used in the microwave?

_____

24. Explain how to vent plastic wrap when using it to cover a dish for microwaving. Why is venting needed?

_____

_____

25. What procedure should be used to prevent overcooking microwaved foods?

_____

_____

26. Why should you use potholders to handle containers of microwaved food?

_____

27. Why should spills and spatters in the microwave be wiped up immediately?

_____

_____

CHAPTER **15** Microwave Techniques   **Text Pages 100-107**

   Microwave Countdown

Directions: Count across the rows of the puzzle below to find every third letter. When you get to each third letter, cross it out and write it on the lines provided below until you have enough letters to form a word related to microwave cookery. (An example has been done to get you started.) After you finish the last row, go back to the first row and continue counting the letters that are not crossed out. If you count correctly, you will spell out seven terms from Chapter 15. When you have found all the terms and written them on the lines below, define each term or explain how it is used in microwave cooking. Some terms are more than one word in length.

M	E_1	T_2	I_3	C_1	O_2	C_3	E	I	R
A	F	O	N	K	W	N	G	A	N
R	V	R	D	E	A	I	S	T	I
C	N	I	O	S	G	O	N	E	K
S	C	I	G	H	N	R	P	G	A
T	P	T	P	O	T	I	W	E	P
E	I	D	R	M	O	A	S	N	R

1. MI _____

   _____

2. _____

   _____

3. _____

   _____

4. _____

   _____

5. _____

   _____

6. _____

   _____

7. _____

Name _____ **Date** _____ **Class Hour** _____

CHAPTER 15 Microwave Techniques **Text Pages 100-107**

The Microwave File

Directions: The numbers beneath the answer blanks below correspond to the numbers on the drawers of the filing cabinet. Find the file drawer that corresponds with the number below the blank. Then determine which of the letters on the file drawer you need to spell the correct word. Write that letter in the appropriate space. If you think you know the term from the clue alone, use the file drawer numbers to check your accuracy.

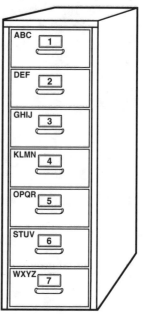

1. This is a major advantage of cooking with a microwave.

‾ ‾ ‾ ‾ ‾ ‾ ‾ ‾ ‾
6 1 6 2 6   6 3 4 2

2. A type of food often made especially for microwave cooking.

‾ ‾ ‾ ‾ ‾ ‾ ‾ ‾ ‾ ‾ ‾
1 5 4 6 2 4 3 2 4 1 2

3. What food molecules do when penetrated by microwaves.

‾ ‾ ‾ ‾ ‾ ‾ ‾
6 3 1 5 1 6 2

4. Materials used in the microwave should have this label.

‾ ‾ ‾ ‾ ‾ ‾ ‾ ‾ ‾ - ‾ ‾ ‾ ‾
4 3 1 5 5 7 1 6 2   6 1 2 2

5. This material should be used in the microwave only when following the manufacturer's recommendations.

‾ ‾ ‾ ‾ ‾ ‾ ‾ ‾ ‾ ‾ ‾ ‾
1 4 6 4 3 4 6 4   2 5 3 4

6. Food cooked in the microwave should be in this kind of pieces.

‾ ‾ ‾ ‾ ‾ ‾ ‾
6 4 3 2 5 5 4

7. Use this to cover food when microwaving if you want to hold in moisture.

‾ ‾ ‾ ‾ ‾ ‾ ‾ ‾ ‾ ‾ ‾
5 4 1 6 6 3 1   7 5 1 5

8. This action will help food heat evenly in the microwave.

‾ ‾ ‾ ‾ ‾ ‾ ‾ ‾ ‾ ‾
5 5 6 1 6 2   2 5 5 2

Discovering Food and Nutrition Student Workbook Protected by Copyright ©

CHAPTER **16** Safety in the Kitchen   **Text Pages 108-113**

Study Guide

Completion: In the space to the left, write the word or words that **BEST** complete(s) each statement.

_____ 1. Cut ___?___ your body when using a knife.

_____ 2. Large pieces of broken glass should be cleaned up with a ___?___.

_____ 3. To pick up tiny pieces of glass, use a ___?___.

_____ 4. When reaching high shelves, use a ___?___.

_____ 5. Rugs in the kitchen should have a ___?___ back.

_____ 6. Electricity and ___?___ are a dangerous pair.

_____ 7. Electrical ___?___ should be kept away from a range or sink.

_____ 8. A damaged electrical cord can be a source of ___?___.

_____ 9. When you disconnect an appliance, hold the ___?___.

_____ 10. Too many appliances plugged into one outlet can cause ___?___ or ___?___.

_____

_____ 11. A source of burns in the kitchen is ___?___.

_____ 12. When cooking, ___?___ clothes can help prevent burns or fires.

_____ 13. Materials that burn easily are called ___?___.

_____ 14. Pan handles should be turned to the ___?___ of the range when cooking.

_____ 15. Using a wet potholder can cause ___?___.

_____ 16. When lifting the cover from a hot pan, uncover the ___?___ of the pan first.

_____ 17. Grease will spatter and burn you if ___?___ is poured on a grease fire.

_____ 18. A grease fire can be put out with the ingredients ___?___ or ___?___.

_____

Continued on next page

_____ 19. Putting a cover on a pan with a grease fire will ___?___ the fire.

_____ 20. When using a household chemical indoors you can ___?___ and ___?___
to prevent the buildup of harmful fumes.

_____

Short Answer: Answer the following questions on the lines provided.

21. What are five common kitchen accidents?

_____

_____

22. Describe how to wash knives safely. Why is this method a safe one?

_____

_____

23. Why should a spill on the floor be wiped up right away?

_____

_____

24. Describe what to do if food gets stuck in an appliance.

_____

_____

25. Name three ways poisoning can occur.

_____

26. Why should you buy only the amount you need of a household chemical?

_____

_____

27. What is the reason for wearing rubber gloves or a mask when using some household chemicals?

_____

_____

28. Describe precautions that should be taken before using a pesticide in the kitchen.

_____

_____

CHAPTER 16 Safety in the Kitchen

   ## Safety Errors

Directions: Read the scenario below. In the chart, write eight safety errors that Nina made, the type of accident that could have been caused, and what she should have done instead.

Nina was making tacos for supper. She needed the largest skillet for the taco meat, so she climbed on a kitchen chair to reach it. While the meat was browning, she covered it. Then she checked its progress by tipping the cover toward her to look at the meat. When Nina went to take the pan from the burner, she realized the potholder was damp, but she didn't have a dry one handy, so she used it anyway. Nina then drained the grease from the browned meat. She spilled some of the grease on the floor, but was in too much of a hurry to wipe it up. Nina spilled the grease because the skillet handle was loose. She used a utility knife to tighten the loose screw on the handle. After she finished cooking the meat, Nina started preparing the other taco ingredients. She cut toward herself when using the knife to peel the tomato. She opened a can of black olives about half way, then bent back the lid and removed the olives for slicing. She chopped the onions and lettuce and grated the cheese. Nina ran a sink of dishwater and put the knife, cutting board, grater, and other equipment she had used into the dishwater.

Safety Error Nina Made	Type of Accident	What Should Nina Have Done?
1.		
2.		
3.		
4.		
5.		
6.		
7.		
8.		

CHAPTER 16 **Safety in the Kitchen**   **Text Pages 108-113**

   Safe or Unsafe?

Directions: Given below are 35 statements describing actions in the kitchen. Read each statement. Decide whether the statement describes a safe or an unsafe action. If the statement is a safe action, shade in the box with the same number in the square below. If the statement is an unsafe action, leave the box with the same number blank. If you correctly identify the safe and unsafe actions, the shaded squares will tell you the number of ways poisoning can occur.

1	2	3	4	5
6	7	8	9	10
11	12	13	14	15
16	17	18	19	20
21	22	23	24	25
26	27	28	29	30
31	32	33	34	35

1. Carry a pan that contains a grease fire to the sink.

2. Sweep up broken glass with a broom or brush.

3. Wait until a wet floor dries before walking on it.

4. Take broken appliances to a service shop for repair.

5. Be sure poisons are clearly labeled.

6. Use a towel to remove a pan from the range.

7. Cut the tops of cans about half off and bend them up to remove food.

8. Keep pan handles toward the edge of the range so they are easy to reach.

9. Touch the electric surface unit on the range after use to be sure it is turned off.

10. Cover food and utensils before spraying with a pesticide.

11. Use a knife to tighten the loose screws on a handle.

12. Wash knives with the silverware when doing dishes.

Continued on next page

13. Store household cleaners in the same cabinets with food.

14. Lift the cover off a pan on the range so the opening is toward you.

15. Keep flammable materials away from the range.

16. Hold onto the cord and tug when disconnecting an appliance.

17. First disconnect an appliance when food is stuck in it.

18. Be sure pot holders are dry before using on hot pans.

19. Put a cover on a pan that holds a grease fire.

20. Be sure kitchen rugs have non-skid backs.

21. Use electric appliances with wet or dry hands.

22. Wear long-sleeved garments when cooking to protect your arms from burns.

23. Use a chair or box to reach a high shelf.

24. Use aerosol spray cans near heat or flames.

25. Cut away from your body when using a knife.

26. Mix household cleaners if dirt is difficult to remove.

27. Clean the range while it is still hot or warm so the food will come off more easily.

28. Pour water on a grease fire.

29. Run electrical cords under rugs so people won't trip over them.

30. Don't plug too many appliance cords into one electrical outlet.

31. Store poisons in empty food or beverage containers.

32. Tie back long hair.

33. Use a wet paper towel to pick up tiny pieces of glass.

34. Pour salt or baking soda over the flames of grease fires.

35. Wipe up spills on the floor right away.

36. What is the number of ways poisoning can occur as shown in the square?

_____

37. What are the three ways poison can enter the body?

_____

CHAPTER 16 Safety in the Kitchen

   ## What's the Word?

Directions: The purpose of kitchen safety is to avoid the word inside the dark lines below. To discover what it is, read each clue below. Write the word or words that fit the clue on the corresponding line of the puzzle, one letter in each box.

1.
2.
3.
4.
5.
6.
7.
8.

Clues

1. A material that burns easily.

2. This can cause severe shocks and burns.

3. The kind of cabinet where household chemicals should be stored in a family with children.

4. An accident that can result from using dangerous chemicals.

5. Use this to reach items on high shelves.

6. One cause of many kitchen burns.

7. The kind of backing a rug used in the kitchen should have.

8. A poison that kills insects and other pests.

9. The word is _____.

Study Guide

Completion: In the space to the left, write the word or words that **BEST** complete(s) each statement.

_____ 1. ___?___ means illness caused by food that is not safe to eat.

_____ 2. The illness called ___?___ is an example of food poisoning.

_____ 3. Living things seen only through a microscope are called ___?___.

_____ 4. Harmful bacteria are also known as ___?___.

_____ 5. Bacteria need ___?___, ___?___, and ___?___ to grow and multiply.

_____

_____

_____ 6. Temperatures between 60°F and 125°F (16°C and 52°C) are in the ___?___ zone.

_____ 7. Most bacteria are killed by temperatures over ___?___.

_____ 8. Bacteria are slowed down by ___?___ temperatures.

_____ 9. Foods that spoil easily are called ___?___.

_____ 10. A refrigerator temperature of ___?___ helps prevent bacteria growth.

_____ 11. The temperature of the freezer should be ___?___ or below.

_____ 12. A ___?___, ___?___, and ___?___ area is needed for dry storage.

_____

_____

_____ 13. Using the ___?___ food first helps save food and money.

_____ 14. Keeping harmful bacteria down to a small number is called ___?___.

_____ 15. Frozen food should NEVER be thawed at ___?___.

_____ 16. Bacteria are carried on ___?___ from pets.

Continued on next page

_____ 17. The garbage can should be emptied ___?___.

_____ 18. Pests will be attracted to discarded containers that contain ___?___.

_____ 19. Long hair should be ___?___ during cooking.

_____ 20. An open wound on the hands should be covered with ___?___.

_____ 21. Harmful bacteria from raw food getting into ready-to-eat food is called ___?___.

_____ 22. ___?___ a cutting board thoroughly after contact with raw meat, poultry, or fish.

Short Answer: Answer the following questions on the lines provided.

23. What are three products that are made with "helpful" bacteria?

_____

_____

24. How do bacteria travel and move about?

_____

_____

25. What are three benefits of proper food storage?

_____

_____

26. Give five examples of perishable foods.

_____

27. How should food be packaged for storage in the freezer?

_____

_____

28. In what order should you store foods when you have been grocery shopping?

_____

_____

29. Why should a hand towel not be used for wiping dishes?

_____

_____

CHAPTER 17 Keeping Food Safe to Eat   **Text Pages 114-121**

Food Storage

Directions: Read the case example described below. Then answer the questions on the lines provided.

Danielle has just come home from the supermarket with the following items: fresh tomatoes, a head of cabbage, a package of macaroni, a bag of marshmallows, a carton of milk, three cans of soup, a carton of ice cream, fresh pears, a can of frozen grape juice, a package of ground beef, a box of frozen green beans, a carton of eggs, a carton of yogurt, a box mix for a cake, American cheese slices, and a box of breakfast cereal.

1. What foods should be stored first?

_____

2. Where should these items be stored?

_____

3. What foods should be stored next?

_____

4. Where should these items be stored?

_____

5. What foods should be stored next?

_____

6. Where should these items be stored?

_____

7. What foods should be stored last?

_____

8. Where should these items be stored?

_____

CHAPTER 17 Keeping Food Safe to Eat   **Text Pages 114-121**

 Food Safety

Directions: What illness will you avoid if you work to keep food safe to eat? To discover the answer, write the word or phrase for each question in the blanks to the left. Place one letter in each blank. Write the circled letters in the appropriate spaces in #14 below.

1. Ⓞ __ __ __ __ __ __   Temperatures at which bacteria multiply very slowly.

2. __ Ⓞ __ __ __ __ __ __   Bacteria need this to grow.

3. __ __ __ Ⓞ __ __ __ __ __ __ __   One illness caused by unsafe food.

4. Ⓞ __ __ __ __ __ __ __ __ __   Range of temperatures at which bacteria grow very rapidly.

5. __ __ __ Ⓞ __ __ __ __ __ __ __ __   These should be stored in a cool, dry place.

6. __ __ Ⓞ __ __ __   What you should wear if you have a wound on your hands.

7. __ __ Ⓞ __ __ __   Wipe up these right away.

8. __ __ __ Ⓞ __ -   This spreads harmful bacteria from raw to ready-to-eat food.

__ __ __ __ __ __ __ __ __ __ __ __ __ __ __

9. __ __ __ __ __ __ __ __ __ Ⓞ __   One place to thaw frozen food.

10. __ __ __ __ Ⓞ __ __   A location for dry storage.

11. __ __ Ⓞ __ __ __ __ __ __ __   Foods that spoil easily.

12. __ __ __ __ __ __ __ __ Ⓞ __   Keeping the number of bacteria down.

13. __ __ __ __ __ __ Ⓞ __   This spoon should be washed before it is used again.

14. __ __ __ __ __ __ __ __ __ __ __ __ __
   1   2   3   4   5   6   7   8   9 10 11 12 13

Study Guide

Completion: In the space to the left, write the word or words that **BEST** complete(s) each statement.

_____ 1. Good ___?___ skills are needed for successful food preparation.

_____ 2. Food labels, newspapers, magazines, family, and friends are good sources of ___?___.

_____ 3. A simple recipe is a good choice to prepare when you have a shortage of ___?___ and ___?___.

_____

_____ 4. Using foods that are on sale when preparing meals helps save ___?___.

_____ 5. A list of what to do to prepare food is called a(n) ___?___.

_____ 6. Getting food or equipment ready for use in a recipe is called ___?___.

_____ 7. A ___?___ will help you plan so the food will be ready when you want to eat it.

_____ 8. The first step in preparing a recipe is to be sure the work area is ___?___.

_____ 9. You can work without being interrupted if you gather the ___?___ and ___?___ you need first.

_____

_____ 10. Using equipment properly helps you keep from wasting ___?___.

_____ 11. ___?___ is working on two or more food preparation steps at the same time.

_____ 12. You can clean up as you go along by having hot, soapy water in your ___?___ or ___?___.

_____

_____ 13. Soaking a pan in ___?___ will help remove any food that is stuck to the bottom.

_____ 14. Items that are greasy should be washed ___?___ other dishes.

_____ 15. The key to success in the foods lab is ___?___.

Continued on next page

_____ 16. Food prepared in the foods lab is rated on ___?___, ___?___, and ___?___.

_____

_____

Short Answer: Answer the following questions on the lines provided.

17. What are three management skills that can be used in food preparation?

_____

_____

18. Name four sources of recipes.

_____

_____

19. What are three examples of pre-preparation tasks?

_____

_____

20. Explain how to use a work plan to make a time schedule.

_____

_____

_____

21. Why is it always important to follow rules of safety and cleanliness when preparing food?

_____

_____

22. Name four cleanup jobs to complete after food has been prepared and eaten.

_____

_____

23. In what order should dishes be washed?

_____

_____

CHAPTER 18 Getting Organized

   Planning Ahead

Directions: Read the recipe below. Then answer the questions on the lines provided.

Grilled Apple-Cheese Sandwiches

Customary	Ingredients	Metric
1 cup	Sharp cheddar cheese, grated	250 mL
1 cup	Apple, finely chopped	250 mL
½ cup	Stuffed green olives, minced	125 mL
⅓ cup	Mayonnaise	75 mL
8 slices	Whole-wheat bread	8 slices
¼ cup	Butter or margarine	50 mL

Yield: 4 sandwiches

Pan: Non-stick griddle

Directions

1. **Combine** cheese, apple, olives, and mayonnaise in mixing bowl.
2. **Spread** mixture on four slices of bread.
3. **Top** with the other four slices of bread.
4. **Spread** butter or margarine on both outer sides of sandwiches.
5. **Heat** griddle over medium heat until a drop of water sizzles when splashed on the griddle.
6. **Grill** sandwiches for 2 to 3 minutes
7. **Turn** over and grill 2 to 3 more minutes until bread is golden brown and cheese is melted.
8. **Serve** immediately.

---

1. List three pre-preparation tasks for this recipe and the equipment needed to complete them.

   _____

   _____

   _____

2. Estimate how long (A) pre-preparation, (B) preparation, and (C) cooking time will take.

   (A) _____ (B) _____ (C) _____

3. How long do you estimate this recipe will take to prepare? _____

4. When should you start cooking to have the sandwiches ready to eat at 6:30 p.m.? _____

5. Which two steps listed above could be dovetailed? Explain. _____

   _____

   _____

CHAPTER 18 **Getting Organized**   **Text Pages 122-127**

 Kitchen Code

Directions: The answers to the following questions from the chapter are in code. Use the example and the questions to break the code. Then decode the mystery message in number 10.

Example: <u>K</u> <u>I</u> <u>T</u> <u>C</u> <u>H</u> <u>E</u> <u>N</u>   <u>C</u> <u>O</u> <u>D</u> <u>E</u>
            G E P Y D A J   Y K Z A

1. _ _ _ _ _ _ _ _ _   What is a resource needed for food preparation?
   A M Q E L I A J P

2. _ _ _ _ _ _ _ _   What is a list of the jobs to be done in food preparation?
   S K N G L H W J

3. _ _ _ _ _ _ _ _ _ _ _ _   What tells you what time to start food preparation?
   P E I A O Y D A Z Q H A

4. _ _ _ _ _   What should you set to help you remember how long
   P E I A N   food should be cooked?

5. _ _ _ _ _ _ _ _ _ _ _   What is it called when you work on two tasks at the
   Z K R A P W E H E J C   same time?

6. _ _ _ _ _ _ _ _   What should be used to rinse dishes?
   D K P S W P A N

7. _ _ _ _ _ _ _ _   What is the key to success when working in the
   P A W I S K N G   foods lab?

8. _ _ _ _ _ _ _ _ _ _ _ _ _ What must each person in a group take?
   N A O L K J O E X E H E P U

9. _ _ _ _ _ _ _ _ _   What is the final step to take to complete lab work?
   A R W H Q W P E K J

10. _ _ _ _ _ _ _ _ _ _ _ _ _ _ _ _ _
    C K K Z I W J W C A I A J P H A W Z O

    _ _ _ _ _ _ _ _ _ _ _ _ _
    P K O Q Y Y A O O E J P D A

    _ _ _ _ _ _ .
    G E P Y D A J

CHAPTER 19 Conserving and Recycling   **Text Pages 128-133**

Study Guide

Completion: In the space to the left, write the word or words that **BEST** complete(s) each statement.

_____ 1. ___?___ fuel helps make sure there will be a future supply.

_____ 2. Appliances that are ___?___ and ___?___ use fuel efficiently.

_____

_____ 3. ___?___ appliances often use less fuel than the rangetop or oven.

_____ 4. The heat is on ___?___ when you use the top of the range.

_____ 5. Cook an entire meal in the oven at the same time to make the most of ___?___.

_____ 6. Water supplies in some communities are ruined by ___?___.

_____ 7. A dishwasher should be run when it is ___?___.

_____ 8. Using too much ___?___ or ___?___ can pollute the water supply.

_____

_____ 9. Buy detergents or other cleaners that do not contain ___?___.

_____ 10. ___?___ in colored paper towels pollutes water.

_____ 11. Water can be polluted by leftover household chemicals that leak in ___?___.

_____ 12. Household chemicals should not be poured down the ___?___.

_____ 13. Buy only the amount of food you will use before it ___?___.

_____ 14. Serving ___?___ portions of food and taking seconds helps prevent food waste.

_____ 15. ___?___ is used to make most plastics.

_____ 16. Most communities use ___?___ or ___?___ to dispose of trash.

_____

Continued on next page

_____ 17. Products used once or only a few times are called ___?___.

_____ 18. In cleanup, a ___?___ can be substituted for a paper towel.

_____ 19. About 50% of trash is ___?___.

_____ 20. Glass jars and covers are useful for ___?___ food.

_____ 21. In ___?___, materials from old products are used to manufacture new items.

_____ 22. Containers to be recycled should be ___?___ to remove food.

Short Answer: Answer the following questions on the lines provided.

23. What are two benefits of using less fuel and two ways to conserve it?

_____

_____

24. Which usually cooks more efficiently, the oven or the rangetop? Why?

_____

_____

25. How should you dispose of leftover household chemicals?

_____

_____

26. What are two benefits of reducing the amount of trash produced in the United States?

_____

27. What are the three Rs of conservation? What are some ways young people can participate in these?

_____

28. How can you reduce the amount of consumer packaging you waste?

_____

_____

29. What are the advantages of buying recycled items as much as possible?

_____

_____

CHAPTER **19** Conserving and Recycling

Text Pages 128-133

   ## Conserving and Recycling

Directions: Read the story below about Jeremy and his mother. On the lines below, suggest 10 ways that Jeremy and his mother could conserve or recycle resources.

"We're out of milk," called Jeremy to his mother as he tossed the plastic milk jug in the waste basket. His mother came into the kitchen and said, "I'll have to run to the supermarket before supper to get some. I just went to the store last night—I wish I'd gotten it then." As his mother got her keys and purse, Jeremy peeked in the oven and asked, "What's for dinner?" His mother said, "Meatloaf," as she went out the door. Jeremy held the oven door open for a couple of minutes, being warmed by the heat. He decided to get a drink of water. He turned on the water so it would cool and got a paper cup to drink from. As he filled the cup, he spilled some water on the floor. He got out a roll of pink plaid paper towels and wiped up the water. Soon his mother was home with the grocery bag. She had a jug of milk and a box of frozen corn for supper. After she took the groceries out of the bag, she gave it to Jeremy to throw away. "Will you set the table, Jeremy?" she said, "and I'll get the potatoes and corn cooking on the rangetop."

1. _____

2. _____

3. _____

4. _____

5. _____

6. _____

7. _____

_____

8. _____

_____

9. _____

_____

10. _____

_____

CHAPTER 19 Conserving and Recycling   **Text Pages 128-133**

   Conserve Your Resources

Directions: Listed below are clues that relate to conserving resources. Use each clue to complete the blank spaces in the corresponding numbered item.

1.   ___ ___ **C** ___ ___ ___ ___ ___ ___

2.   ___ ___ **O** ___ ___ ___ ___

3.   ___ ___ **N** ___ ___ ___ ___ ___

4.   ___ ___ ___ **S** ___ ___ ___

5.   ___ ___ ___ **E** ___ ___ ___ ___ ___

6. ___ ___ ___ **R** ___ ___ ___ ___ ___ ___

7.   ___ **V** ___ ___

8.   ___ **E** ___ ___ ___ ___ ___

Clues

1. This makes up a large portion of trash.

2. This can create a water shortage.

3. A place where trash is normally buried.

4. This is made from petroleum.

5. This can pollute water if too much is used.

6. This will be improved by conserving and recycling.

7. The most fuel-efficient part of the range.

8. When people do this, new products are made from the materials of old ones.

Study Guide

Completion: In the space to the left, write the word or words that **BEST** complete(s) each statement.

_____ 1. Using basic management skills in preparing good meals is called ___?___.

_____ 2. The first step in meal management is ___?___ the meal.

_____ 3. A list of foods to serve at a meal is a(n) ___?___.

_____ 4. When meal planning, start by selecting a(n) ___?___.

_____ 5. The number and kinds of foods included in a meal plan depends on the ___?___ of those eating the meal.

_____ 6. When planning menus, choose nutritious foods from the ___?___ main food groups in the Food Guide Pyramid.

_____ 7. The ___?___ used in meal planning include time, money, and skills.

_____ 8. Foods that look and taste good have meal ___?___.

_____ 9. A combination of foods with strong and mild tastes provide a variety of ___?___.

_____ 10. A variety of ___?___ adds visual appeal to meals.

_____ 11. Whether a food is crunchy or tender is called ___?___.

_____ 12. All foods for a meal should be ready at the right ___?___.

_____ 13. A(n) ___?___-step process is used in planning for meal preparation.

_____ 14. A combined ___?___ is the basis for a time schedule for preparing a meal.

_____ 15. The recipe or package direction usually give ___?___ time.

_____ 16. In making a work plan for a meal, the cook chooses the best ___?___ in which to prepare foods.

_____ 17. Baking a casserole while you prepare a salad is an example of ___?___.

_____ 18. If more than one person is fixing a meal, each one should have specific ___?___ to do.

Continued on next page

_____ 19. When making a time schedule for meal preparation, set the time to serve the meal and work ___?___.

_____ 20. Spending time to ___?___ ahead will help meal preparation go more smoothly.

Short Answer: Answer the following questions on the lines provided.

21. What are two important factors in preparing a successful meal?

_____

_____

22. What are three management skills useful in meal management?

_____

_____

23. How should nutrition be considered when planning meals?

_____

_____

24. Suggest three garnishes that will add color to food.

_____

25. Identify three ways foods can be cut to add interest to a meal.

_____

26. In identifying the preparation tasks for each food on your menu, what three column headings should you use?

_____

_____

27. Name four basic tasks that need to be included in making a task list for every meal.

_____

_____

28. What could be done when there are two preparation tasks that require your full attention at the same time?

_____

CHAPTER 20 Meal Management   **Text Pages 134-139**

Meal Manager

Dear Meal Manager,
~~~~~~~~~~~~~~~~
~~~~~~~~~~~~~~~~
~~~~~~~~~~~~~~~~
~~~~~~~~~~~~~~~~
~~~~~~~~~~~~~~~~
~~~~~~~~~~~~~~~~
~~~~~~~~~~~~~~~~

Signed,
~~~~~~~

Directions: Assume you are a newspaper columnist called *Meal Manager*. Read the following letters you have received and write your answers to the letters on the lines provided.

1. Dear Meal Manager:

   My brother and I fix meals together, but we always fight. We try to help each other, but he'll have the knife I need or I've already done what he is doing. Is there any way for us to work together?

   Signed,
   War in the Kitchen

   _____

   _____

   _____

2. Dear Meal Manager:

   I'm supposed to cook supper one night a week when my mom has to work late. I don't ever manage to get everything ready at the same time—something is always burned, or cold, or only half cooked. How can I get things ready at the same time?

   Signed,
   Frustrated

   _____

   _____

   _____

3. Dear Meal Manager:

   My favorite meal is scalloped potatoes and ham, applesauce, cauliflower, and french bread. Everyone groans when I fix it for supper. Why does no one else like it?

   Signed,
   Puzzled

   _____

   _____

   _____

CHAPTER 20 Meal Management   **Text Pages 134-139**

Call for Successful Meal Planning

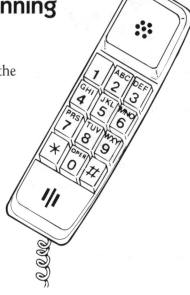

Directions: The numbers beneath the answer blanks below correspond to the numbers on the telephone buttons. There are three letters on each button (except the buttons marked 1 and 0). Decide which of the three letters on the indicated button is used in each answer. Write the correct letters in the spaces. If you decide on an answer from the clue alone, use the numbers to check your accuracy.

1. __ __ __ __ __ __ __ __
  7 5 2 6 6 4 6 4

Management skill used in preparing successful meals.

2. __ __ __ __
  6 3 6 8

A list of foods to serve at a meal.

3. __ __ __ __ __ __ __ __ __
  6 8 8 7 4 8 4 6 6

A factor to consider in planning meals.

4. __ __ __ __ __ __ __
  8 2 9 8 8 7 2

Whether a food is hard or soft.

5. __ __ __ __ __
  7 5 4 5 5

An example of a resource used in meal planning.

6. __ __ __ __ __ __ __
  3 5 2 8 6 7 7

A variety of these are needed at each meal.

7. __ __ __ __ __
  2 6 5 6 7

Garnishes add this to a meal.

8. __ __ __ __   __ __ __ __
  9 6 7 5   7 5 2 6

Coordinating meal preparation is easier with this.

9. __ __ __ __   __ __ __ __ __ __ __
  6 3 2 5   7 2 8 8 3 7 6 7

People's preferences for eating specific foods at specific times of day.

Study Guide

Completion: In the space to the left, write the word or words that **BEST** complete(s) each statement.

_____ 1. In ___?___ food is placed in serving dishes on the table.

_____ 2. In ___?___ food is brought to the table on each person's plate.

_____ 3. ___?___ is needed to serve and eat food.

_____ 4. Foods such as cereal and soup are served in ___?___.

_____ 5. Large bowls and platters are called ___?___.

_____ 6. A glass that has a stem between the base and bowl is called ___?___.

_____ 7. Glasses without stems are called ___?___.

_____ 8. ___?___ is a term for knives, forks, and spoons.

_____ 9. A small fork is often used for ___?___ or ___?___.

_____

_____ 10. A spoon with a large bowl is used for eating ___?___.

_____ 11. Napkins, placemats, and tablecloths are called ___?___.

_____ 12. A(n) ___?___ is the arrangement of tableware for each person.

_____ 13. A plate should be placed about ___?___ from the table's edge.

_____ 14. The fork(s) goes to the ___?___ of the plate.

_____ 15. The flatware farthest from the plate is what you use ___?___.

_____ 16. The knife and spoon go to the ___?___ of the plate.

_____ 17. The ___?___ of the knife faces the plate.

_____ 18. Just above the tip of the knife, place the ___?___.

_____ 19. The salad plate goes above the ___?___.

Continued on next page

_____ 20. To the left of the forks, place the ___?___.

_____ 21. Table manners are based on ___?___ for others.

_____ 22. During the meal the napkin should be ___?___.

_____ 23. ___?___ is placed in the center of the plate when you are finished eating.

Short Answer: Answer the following questions on the lines provided.

24. Why do families have specific customs for serving meals?

_____

_____

25. Why are some foods served on smaller separate plates instead of on a dinner plate?

_____

_____

26. What is the basic rule about using flatware?

_____

_____

27. Describe how to place the napkin on the table when there is plenty of room. Why should it be put this way?

_____

_____

28. Why is good conversation important at mealtime?

_____

_____

29. When should you begin eating when you are with a small group?

_____

_____

30. When can you eat foods with your fingers?

_____

Discovering Food and Nutrition Student Workbook Protected by Copyright ©

CHAPTER 21 **Serving a Meal**   **Text Pages 140-145**

   ## Hidden Tableware

Directions: Fifteen different items of tableware are hidden in the puzzle below. They are printed forward, backward, horizontally, and vertically. Circle each item if tableware. Decide what type of tableware it is and list it under the appropriate type in the chart below.

```
U   I   T   T   A   B   L   E   C   L   O   T   H
D   S   E   C   O   N   H   J   U   P   L   T   G
I   T   A   M   E   C   A   L   P   S   R   V   U
N   M   S   B   R   E   T   T   A   L   P   B   M
N   F   P   E   I   J   M   K   N   I   F   E   R
E   E   O   A   W   T   E   S   D   K   B   C   L
R   R   O   U   S   O   U   P   S   P   O   O   N
P   A   N   K   Y   S   C   E   A   T   W   E   A
L   W   G   R   E   L   B   M   U   T   L   N   P
A   M   R   O   D   N   I   U   C   E   F   I   K
T   E   A   F   B   T   A   L   E   T   T   L   I
E   T   A   L   P   D   A   E   R   B   O   G   N
L   S   Z   Q   U   E   M   A   F   I   C   P   S
```

Plates	Other Dishes	Glasses	Flatware	Linens

CHAPTER 21 **Serving a Meal**   **Text Pages 140-145**

 Place Settings

Directions: On the placemat below, draw a place setting with each tableware item in the correct position. Label each item with its number.

1. dinner plate   2. salad plate   3. water glass   4. milk glass   5. cup and saucer

6. knife   7. dinner fork   8. salad fork   9. teaspoon   10. napkin

Directions: You are serving the menu listed below. Decide which tableware item or items your guests would use to eat each food. Write the numbers of the tableware needed next to each food item. Use the numbers from the place setting above.

Menu

_____ 11. Broiled lamb chop

_____ 12. Twice baked potato

_____ 13. Winter squash casserole

_____ 14. Tossed salad

_____ 15. Dark rye dinner rolls

_____ 16. Lemon cake with ice cream

_____ 17. Milk

CHAPTER 22 Packing a Lunch   **Text Pages 146-149**

Study Guide

Completion: In the space to the left, write the word or words that **BEST** complete(s) each statement.

_____   1. When you eat a packed lunch, it should be ___?___ and in good condition.

_____   2. The ___?___ should be used to plan a nutritious packed lunch.

_____   3. Harmful ___?___ can grow in food that is not kept hot or cold enough.

_____   4. An insulated bottle that keeps foods at their original temperatures is called a(n) ___?___.

_____   5. Beverages are carried in ___?___ vacuum bottles.

_____   6. Hot foods are carried in ___?___ vacuum bottles.

_____   7. The best vacuum bottle linings for keeping foods hot are ___?___ or
_____   ___?___.

_____   8. Using ___?___ will help heat a vacuum bottle before filling it with hot food.

_____   9. Until you are ready to pack your lunch in the morning, keep cold foods in
_____   the ___?___ or ___?___.

_____   10. A reusable ___?___ gel pack will help keep sandwiches cold.

_____   11. A(n) ___?___ sandwich will help keep other foods cold.

_____   12. A(n) ___?___ bag can help keep food cold.

_____   13. Using ___?___ can help you come up with interesting food combinations for packed lunches.

_____   14. To keep packed food fresh, use ___?___ wrappings or containers.

_____   15. To avoid wasting materials, you can pack food in reusable ___?___ containers.

_____   16. To get rid of food odors in plastic containers, ___?___ them.

Continued on next page

_____ 17. Some foods for packed lunches can be prepared the ___?___.

_____ 18. Fresh vegetables for your sandwich should be packed ___?___.

Short Answer: Answer the following questions on the lines provided.

19. What are four characteristics of a good packed lunch?

_____

20. What foods should a packed lunch contain for good nutrition?

_____

21. What are the advantages of using a vacuum bottle in a packed lunch?

_____

_____

22. Describe how to preheat and prechill a vacuum bottle.

_____

_____

_____

23. What are two advantages of including a frozen sandwich in your lunch?

_____

_____

24. Name three ways to keep packed food fresh. Which of these is the best way? Why?

_____

_____

_____

25. How should a lunchbox be cared for?

_____

_____

_____

CHAPTER 22 **Packing a Lunch**

Annie's Advice

Directions: Assume that you are a food consultant named Annie. You help people with food problems. Read the letters you have received below and write your responses on the lines provided.

1. Dear Annie:

   I would rather take my lunch to school but I never seem to have time to pack it in the morning. I barely have time to grab some breakfast. How can I find time to make lunch?

   Signed,
   Sleeps Too Late

   _____

   _____

2. Dear Annie:

   I often carry fruit or salad in a plastic container. Lately I've noticed it has started to smell of food. Is there any way I can get rid of the smell?

   Signed,
   Nosy

   _____

   _____

3. Dear Annie:

   I love sandwiches with mayonnaise, meat, lettuce, tomatoes, sprouts, and other good vegetables on them. However, by lunch time the bread is so soggy I can't eat it. How can I prevent this from happening?

   Signed,
   Hates Soggy Sandwiches

   _____

   _____

4. Dear Annie:

   I often make a week's worth of sandwiches on the weekend and freeze them. This week I froze tuna and egg salad sandwiches. When I took them to school, they were awful! What did I do wrong?

   Signed,
   Threw Them Out

   _____

   _____

CHAPTER 22 Packing a Lunch   **Text Pages 146-149**

Magic Lunch Square

Directions: Find the term that best fits each description. Write the number of the correct term in the space in each lettered square. If all your answers are correct, the total of the numbers, or the "Magic Number," will be the same in each row across and down. Write the Magic Number in the space provided.

Terms

1. beverages
2. egg
3. heat outlet
4. illness
5. insulated bag
6. plastic container
7. preheated
8. safe
9. vacuum bottle
10. wide-mouthed

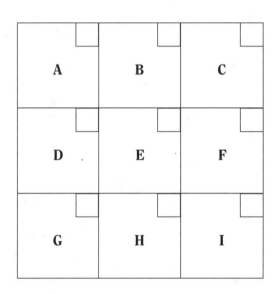

A	B	C
D	E	F
G	H	I

The Magic Number is _____.

Descriptions

A. What can occur if food in a packed lunch is not kept either cold or very hot.
B. This sandwich filling does not freeze well.
C. A container used to keep foods at their original temperature.
D. Avoid storing a packed lunch near this.
E. What should be done to a vacuum bottle before carrying soup in it.
F. This can be used to keep a packed lunch cold.
G. A packed lunch should be this.
H. This helps keep packed food fresh.
I. What is usually carried in a narrow-mouth vacuum bottle.

CHAPTER 23 Milk    **Text Pages 150-157**

Study Guide

Completion: In the space to the left, write the word or words that **BEST** answer(s) each question.

_____   1. How many milk group servings do teens need every day?

_____   2. What nutrient in milk is used for growth and repair of the body?

_____   3. Name one nutrient found in milk needed for strong bones and teeth?

_____   4. Which type of fresh milk contains the most fat?

_____   5. What type of fresh milk has almost all of its fat removed?

_____   6. What 2 types of milk are best for a healthy diet?

_____

_____   7. What type of milk should children younger than two drink?

_____   8. Where is fresh milk found in the supermarket?

_____   9. How has UHT milk been processed?

_____   10. What type of milk can be used in place of cream?

_____   11. What is added in making sweetened condensed milk?

_____   12. What type of milk comes in powdered form?

_____   13. How are bacteria killed during pasteurization?

_____   14. What vitamin is always added to low-fat and skim milk?

_____   15. In what type of container should fresh milk be stored?

_____   16. Where should fresh milk be stored?

_____   17. In what kind of container should opened dry milk be stored?

_____   18. At what temperature should milk be cooked?

_____   19. What causes milk to scorch?

Continued on next page

_____ 20. What does milk do when it separates into lumps and a liquid?

_____ 21. What kind of sauce is created when milk is thickened with flour?

_____ 22. In what type of cooking method is milk least likely to scorch?

Short Answer: Answer the following questions on the lines provided.

23. What does it mean when the label says fresh milk is homogenized?

_____

24. What does the date on a container of fresh milk mean?

_____

25. Describe the qualities of a properly cooked milk product.

_____

_____

26. The skin that forms on milk that is heated is made of two ingredients of the milk. What are they?

_____

27. Why does milk with a skin on it often boil over? What can be done to prevent this?

_____

_____

_____

28. Why does milk curdle during cooking?

_____

_____

29. List at least two uses for white sauce.

_____

30. Describe how to heat milk in the microwave.

_____

_____

_____

Discovering Food and Nutrition Student Workbook Protected by Copyright ©

Name _____ Date _____ Class Hour_____

CHAPTER 23 Milk

Text Pages 150-157

Milk Matchups

Directions: Match each description in the left column with the correct kind of milk from the right column. Write the letter of the kind of milk in the space provided. Do not use any kind of milk more than once. Some kinds of milk will not be used.

Descriptions

____ 1. Between 22 and 35 percent of calories come from fat.

____ 2. Heated to kill harmful bacteria.

____ 3. Separated into many small lumps and a watery liquid.

____ 4. Has a burnt flavor.

____ 5. Over half its calories come from fat.

____ 6. Has half of its water removed.

____ 7. Vitamins D and sometimes A are added.

____ 8. Fat is mixed permanently with the milk.

____ 9. Concentrated with sugar added.

____ 10. Most of the fat and water are removed.

____ 11. Has only a trace of fat.

____ 12. Processed using extra-high heat.

____ 13. Water that has been removed is replaced.

Kinds of Milk

A. Chocolate

B. Curdled

C. Evaporated

D. Fortified

E. Homogenized

F. Low-fat

G. Nonfat dry

H. Pasteurized

I. Reconstituted

J. Scalded

K. Scorched

L. Skim

M. Sweetened condensed

N. UHT

O. Whole

Name _____ Date _____ Class Hour_____

CHAPTER 23 Milk Text Pages 150-157

   Cooking with Milk

Directions: What is the nutrient in milk that makes it sensitive to heat? To discover the answer, write the word or phrase for each definition or questions in the blanks provided, placing one letter on each blank. Transfer the circled letter to the appropriate blank in #8 below.

1. __ __ __ Ⓞ __   In a sauce, these should be pressed against the side of the container until they disappear.

2. __ __ __ __ __ __ Ⓞ   What milk does if not stirred when heated in the microwave.

3. __ __ Ⓞ __ __   Use this to measure the temperature of milk heated in the microwave.

4. __ __ __ Ⓞ __   A milk-based sauce thickened with flour.

5. __ __ Ⓞ __ __   The kind of texture a cooked milk product should have.

6. __ __ Ⓞ __   This kind of ingredient can cause milk to curdle.

7. __ __ __ Ⓞ __   What milk solids do if cooked at too high a temperature.

8. __ __ __ __ __ __ __

Directions: Milk will have a burnt flavor if not cooked correctly. What is the first step in preventing this? To discover the answer, write the word or phrase for each definition or question on the blanks to its left, placing one letter on each blank. Transfer the circled letters to the appropriate blanks in #19 below.

9. __ __ Ⓞ __ __ __   Milk is often used in recipes for these.

10. Ⓞ __ __ __ __ __   How milk should be cooked.

11. __ __ Ⓞ __ __ __   This is prevented from escaping by a milk skin.

12. __ __ __ __ Ⓞ __ __   What milk does when it separates into tiny lumps and a watery liquid.

13. __ Ⓞ __ __ __ __ __ __   Milk is likely to do this when heated in the microwave.

14. __ __ __ Ⓞ __   What milk skin usually is.

15. __ __ __ __ Ⓞ __ __   Milk that has a burnt flavor.

16. __ __ __ Ⓞ __   This may help prevent a milk skin from forming.

17. __ __ __ Ⓞ __ __ __   The kind of flavor a cooked milk beverage should have.

18. __ __ Ⓞ __   This is part of what makes up a milk skin.

19. __ __ __ __ __ __ __ __ __ __

Study Guide

Completion: In the space to the left, write the word or words that **BEST** complete(s) each statement.

_____ 1. A special ___?___ is added to milk to make yogurt.

_____ 2. Yogurt has a ___?___ flavor and a smooth, thick texture.

_____ 3. The liquid portion of thickened milk is called the ___?___.

_____ 4. Cheese is made from the ___?___ of thickened milk.

_____ 5. Cheese is an important source of vitamins ___?___ and ___?___.

_____

_____ 6. Cheeses that are high in ___?___ should be eaten in moderation.

_____ 7. There are ___?___ general types of cheeses.

_____ 8. Cream cheese is an example of a(n) ___?___ cheese.

_____ 9. Cottage cheese will stay fresh for ___?___ after purchase.

_____ 10. Brick and cheddar are examples of ___?___ cheeses.

_____ 11. Ripened cheeses and other ingredients are used to make ___?___ cheese.

_____ 12. The most common example of process cheese is ___?___.

_____ 13. Ripened cheeses are usually ___?___ in cost than process cheeses.

_____ 14. Cheese that is sliced or shredded usually costs more than the same cheese in ___?___ form.

_____ 15. Yogurt should be stored in ___?___.

_____ 16. Yogurt should be served ___?___.

_____ 17. Yogurt cheese is lower in ___?___ than cream cheese.

_____ 18. Cheese should be cooked at ___?___ temperatures.

Continued on next page

_____ 19. Cheese will melt more evenly if it is ___?___ or ___?___.

_____

_____ 20. Cheese that is overcooked in the microwave is ___?___ and ___?___.

_____

_____ 21. Cheese should be added ___?___ of cooking time.

_____ 22. ___?___ cheese is least likely to overcook in the microwave.

Short Answer: Answer the following questions on the lines provided.

23. Sandra says yogurt is more healthy to eat than cheese. Why does she make this claim?

_____

_____

24. Name at least three types of yogurt that are available.

_____

25. Tara is looking at two different brands of mozzarella cheese. They are in the same sized packages and cost the same. How might she decide between them?

_____

_____

_____

26. Give at least two suggestions for storing a block of cheddar cheese.

_____

_____

27. List at least three foods where cooked cheese adds flavor.

_____

28. How long should cheese be cooked?

_____

29. What two types of cheese are best for cooking?

_____

_____

Discovering Food and Nutrition Student Workbook Protected by Copyright ©

Name _____   Date _____   Class Hour_____

CHAPTER **24** Yogurt and Cheese   Text Pages 158-163

 Cheese Clues

Directions: Hidden in this puzzle are the nine kinds of cheese listed in scrambled form below. Unscramble the letters and then circle the cheese names in the puzzle. Names will appear backwards, forwards, horizontally, and vertically. Then list each cheese in the appropriate column below.

daehdcr _____   necmiraa _____

dareps _____   sissw _____

krcbi _____   tgetoca _____

marce _____   tgyuor _____

meanraps _____

S	O	P	A	R	M	E	S	A	N
W	A	W	M	E	S	M	I	C	R
I	C	H	E	D	D	A	R	V	E
S	P	A	R	A	T	E	R	R	A
S	S	O	I	S	P	R	E	A	D
B	R	I	C	K	O	C	R	E	A
T	E	G	A	T	T	O	C	R	S
S	W	I	N	T	R	U	G	O	Y

1. Unripened   **2. Ripened**   **3. Process**

_____   _____   _____

_____   _____   _____

_____   _____   _____

_____   _____   _____

CHAPTER 24 Yogurt and Cheese   **Text Pages 158-163**

What Would You Buy?

Directions: Read the problems below, make the needed calculations, and answer the questions in the space provided.

1. Natalie plans to serve cheese slices and fruit to her friends after a ball game. When at the supermarket, she can't decide what cheese to buy. She is considering individually wrapped American cheese slices that cost $3.49 for a 16 oz. (454 g) package. She also sees a variety package of sliced cheddar, brick, and Swiss cheese that costs $2.65 for 8 oz. (227 g); a 10 oz. (284 g) block of sharp cheddar that costs $2.75; and an 8 oz. (227 g) package of sliced cheddar that costs $2.49. What is the cost per ounce of each option? What would you buy? Why?

_____ (Show your work here)

_____

_____

_____

2. Gary's family eats a lot of cheese. He usually buys a 16 oz. (454 g) package of shredded cheddar ($3.95) and a 16 oz. (454 g) package of sliced American cheese ($3.49) when he shops. He wonders whether he should start buying a 2 lb. block of American ($6.20) instead. What would you buy? Why?

_____ (Show your work here)

_____

_____

_____

3. Tamika is the only person in her family who likes yogurt. When she is shopping, she finds 8 oz. (227 g) cartons of vanilla yogurt for 83 cents. She notices a large 32 oz. (908 g) carton of vanilla yogurt for $2.49. What is the cost per ounce of each size of the yogurt? What factor other than cost is important in this choice? Which size would you buy? Why?

_____ (Show your work here)

_____

_____

_____

Study Guide

Completion: In the space to the left, write the word or words that **BEST** complete(s) each statement.

_____   1. The kernels or seeds of cereal grasses are known as ___?___.

_____   2. The most important nutrient found in the Bread, Cereal, Rice, and Pasta group is ___?___.

_____   3. Grain products are a source of incomplete ___?___.

_____   4. The ___?___ in grain products helps build healthy red blood cells.

_____   5. There are ___?___ basic parts to a kernel of grain.

_____   6. Products made from the entire kernel of grain are called ___?___.

_____   7. All-purpose white flour is made from the ___?___ of the wheat kernel.

_____   8. When grain is processed to remove the bran and germ, many ___?___ are lost.

_____   9. Grain products with added nutrients are called ___?___.

_____   10. Eating whole-grain products is a good way to add ___?___ to the diet.

_____   11. ___?___ is needed to keep some bagels and English muffins fresh.

_____   12. The rice whose kernels cook dry and fluffy is ___?___.

_____   13. Rice with a nutty flavor and a chewy texture is ___?___ rice.

_____   14. White rice is also called ___?___ rice.

_____   15. Rice that is precooked, rinsed, and dried is called ___?___ rice.

_____   16. The general term for noodles, macaroni, and spaghetti is ___?___.

_____   17. Added ingredients usually make a grain product cost ___?___.

_____   18. Refrigerating bread helps prevent the growth of ___?___.

_____   19. Three cups of cooked rice comes from ___?___ cup(s) raw rice.

Continued on next page

_____ 20. ___?___ are lost when cooked grain products are rinsed.

_____ 21. Rice becomes ___?___ if it is stirred too much.

Short Answer: Answer the following questions on the lines provided.

22. List the three parts of a grain kernel and tell what nutrients each part contains.

_____

_____

_____

23. How does white rice differ nutritionally from brown rice? Why?

_____

_____

24. From what ingredients is pasta made? How do noodles usually differ from other kinds of pasta?

_____

_____

25. What happens to grain products as they cook that causes an increase in size?

_____

26. Describe properly cooked, overcooked, and undercooked grain products.

_____

_____

_____

_____

27. What does the term "al-dente" mean?

_____

28. Why does cooking grain products in the microwave take about as long as cooking them conventionally?

_____

_____

Discovering Food and Nutrition Student Workbook Protected by Copyright ©

CHAPTER 25 **Grain Products**   **Text Pages 164-171**

   Grains and Breads Puzzle

Directions: Listed below are clues that have to do with grains, breads, and a healthful diet. Fill in the letter blanks for each term to complete the puzzle.

1. ___ ___ ___ **G** ___ ___ ___ ___ ___

2. ___ ___ **R** ___ ___ ___ ___ ___

3. ___ ___ ___ **A**

4. ___ **I** **B** ___ ___

5. ___ **N** **R** ___ ___ ___ ___ ___

6. **S** **E** ___ ___ ___

7. ___ **A** ___ ___ ___

8. ___ ___ ___ ___ ___ **D**

9. ___ ___ ___ ___ **S** ___ ___ ___ ___

Clues

1. You increase fat and calories when you serve bread with this.

2. A thin, flat bread made from corn flour or wheat flour.

3. A thick, flat bread with a pocket.

4. Whole-grain breads are a good source of this.

5. Bread that has added iron and B vitamins.

6. Another name for the kernels of cereal grains.

7. A donut-shaped roll with a chewy texture.

8. The way most loaves of bread are sold.

9. All-purpose white flour is made from this.

Name _____ Date _____ Class Hour_____

CHAPTER **25** Grain Products   **Text Pages 164-171**

   ## Reading Cereal Labels

Directions: All ready-to-eat breakfast cereals have nutrition labels called "Nutrition Facts" on their boxes. Two cereal labels are shown here. Read each label and answer the questions on the lines provided.

Cereal A

Nutrition Facts

Serving Size 1 Cup (30g/1.1 oz.)
Servings per Container About 14

Amount Per Serving	Cereal	Cereal with ½ Cup Vitamins A & D Skim Milk
Calories	110	150
Calories from Fat	0	0
	% Daily Value	
Total Fat 0g	0%	0%
Saturated Fat 0g	0%	0%
Cholesterol 0mg	0%	0%
Sodium 135mg	6%	8%
Potassium 30mg	1%	7%
Total Carbohydrate 27g	9%	11%
Dietary Fiber 1g	4%	4%
Sugars 14g		
Other Carbohydrate 12g		
Protein 2g		
Vitamin A	15%	20%
Vitamin C	25%	25%
Calcium	0%	15%
Iron	25%	25%
Vitamin D	10%	25%
Thiamin	25%	30%
Riboflavin	25%	35%
Niacin	25%	25%
Vitamin B$_6$	25%	25%
Folate	25%	25%
Phosphorus	2%	15%
Magnesium	2%	6%
Zinc	25%	25%
Copper	4%	6%

Ingredients: Corn, wheat and oat flour; sugar; salt; dried apples; apple juice concentrate; cinnamon; yellow #6; red #40;
Vitamins and Minerals: sodium ascorbate and ascorbic acid (vitamin C); niacinamide; zinc oxide; iron, pyridoxine hydrochloride (vitamin B$_6$), riboflavin (vitamin B$_2$), vitamin A palmitate (protected with BHT); thiamin hydrochloride (vitamin B$_1$), folic acid, and vitamin D.

Cereal B

Nutrition Facts

Serving Size ¾ Cup (55g/2.0 oz.)
Servings per Container About 10

Amount Per Serving	Cereal	Cereal with ½ Cup Vitamins A & D Skim Milk
Calories	230	270
Calories from Fat	70	70
	% Daily Value	
Total Fat 8g	12%	12%
Saturated Fat 3g	15%	15%
Cholesterol 0mg	0%	0%
Sodium 180mg	8%	10%
Potassium 240mg	7%	13%
Total Carbohydrate 40g	13%	15%
Dietary Fiber 6g	24%	24%
Sugars 18g		
Other Carbohydrate 16g		
Protein 4g		
Vitamin A	15%	20%
Vitamin C	25%	25%
Calcium	2%	15%
Iron	10%	10%
Vitamin D	10%	25%
Thiamin	25%	30%
Riboflavin	25%	35%
Niacin	25%	25%
Vitamin B$_6$	25%	25%
Folate	25%	25%
Phosphorus	20%	30%
Magnesium	20%	25%
Zinc	10%	15%
Copper	8%	10%

Ingredients: Whole oats and oat bran, brown sugar, wheat bran, partially hydrogenated cottonseed and/or soybean oil, corn syrup, sugar, coconut, wheat starch, malt flavoring, cinnamon, salt, baking soda, vanilla extract, nutmeg.
Vitamins and Minerals: sodium ascorbate and ascorbic acid (vitamin C), niacinamide, zinc oxide, iron, pyridoxine hydrochloride (vitamin B$_6$), riboflavin (vitamin B$_2$), vitamin A palmitate, thiamin hydrochloride (vitamin B$_1$), folic acid, and vitamin D.

Continued on next page

Discovering Food and Nutrition Student Workbook Protected by Copyright ©

CHAPTER **25** Grain Products

Text Pages 164-171

 Reading Cereal Labels

1. How big is a serving of cereal A? Cereal B?

_____

2. How do the number of calories in a serving of each cereal compare?

_____

3. How do the number of calories from fat in a serving of each cereal compare?

_____

4. Would either of these cereals eaten alone be a good source of calcium? Why or why not?

_____

_____

5. Which of these cereals is lower in sodium?

_____

6. Which of these cereals is lower in sugar?

_____

_____

7. Which cereal would be better for a low-fat diet? Why?

_____

8. Which cereal would be better for a high-fiber diet? Why?

_____

9. Why should people be encouraged to eat these cereals with milk?

_____

10. Which cereal do you think is a more healthful choice? Why?

_____

_____

CHAPTER 25 Grain Products   **Text Pages 164-171**

▼ ▼ ▼ Cooking Grain Products

Directions: Grain products increase in bulk when they are cooked. Pasta generally swells to double in size while rice triples in size. In answering the following questions, assume that one serving equals 1/2 cup (125 mL).

1. A recipe for a chicken casserole calls for 3 cups (750 mL) cooked noodles. How many cups of uncooked noodles would you need to use?

_____

_____

2. How much uncooked macaroni would be needed to serve ten people?

_____

_____

3. How much uncooked spaghetti would be needed to serve four people?

_____

_____

4. A recipe for a beef casserole calls for 3 cups of cooked rice. How much raw rice would you cook?

_____

_____

5. How much uncooked rice would be needed to serve 12 people?

_____

_____

6. How much uncooked rice would be needed to serve two people?

_____

_____

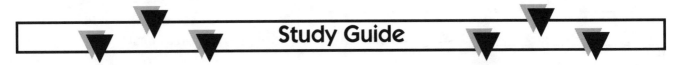

Study Guide

Completion: In the space to the left, write the word or words that **BEST** complete(s) each statement.

_____   1. The ___?___ found in fruit helps digestion.

_____   2. Fruits are good sources of vitamins ___?___ and ___?___.

_____

_____   3. ___?___ is a mineral found in fruit.

_____   4. Fruits are sold in ___?___, ___?___, ___?___, or ___?___ forms.

_____

_____

_____

_____   5. The most nutrients are found in ___?___ fruit in good condition.

_____   6. Tender fruits with full flavor and sweetness are ___?___.

_____   7. Two fruits that stop ripening when they are picked are ___?___ and ___?___.

_____   8. Two fruits that continue to ripen after picking are ___?___ and ___?___.

_____

_____   9. Very soft fruit is probably ___?___ and will lack flavor.

_____   10. Ripe fresh fruits should be stored in ___?___ in the refrigerator.

_____   11. Underripe fresh fruit should be stored in paper bags ___?___.

_____   12. Cut fresh fruit should be stored in a(n) ___?___ container or wrapped in foil or plastic.

_____   13. When buying canned fruits, choose fruit packed in ___?___ or ___?___.

_____

Continued on next page

_____ 14. Leftover canned fruit should be refrigerated in ___?___.

_____ 15. Washing fresh fruit before eating removes ___?___ and ___?___.

_____

_____ 16. Fruits lose vitamin ___?___ when they are pared or cut.

_____ 17. Keep cut bananas looking fresh by coating them with ___?___ juice.

_____ 18. The ___?___ and ___?___ in fruits causes them to cook quickly in the microwave.

_____

Short Answer: Answer the following questions on the lines provided.

19. What are three reasons to include fruit in your diet?

_____

_____

20. Why should you buy only the amount of fresh fruit you can use in a few days?

_____

_____

21. What effect does the time of the year have on fruit prices?

_____

_____

22. Why are low-quality fruits not a good buy?

_____

_____

23. What are five traits of a high-quality fruit?

_____

_____

_____

24. List three ways cooking affects fruit.

_____

_____

CHAPTER 26 Fruits   **Text Pages 172-179**

   ## Choosing Nutritious Fruits

Directions: It is important to consider nutrition when choosing fruit. Listed below are pairs of fruits. Put a check in the blank to the left of the fruit in each pair you think is most healthful. Explain why in the space provided.

1. _____ Frozen strawberries with sugar

   _____ Frozen strawberries without sugar

   Why are the strawberries you checked most healthful?

   _____

   _____

   _____

2. _____ Fresh grapefruit segments

   _____ Canned grapefruit segments

   Why are the grapefruit segments you checked most healthful?

   _____

   _____

   _____

3. _____ Canned peach slices in water

   _____ Canned peach slices in syrup

   Why are the peach slices you checked most healthful?

   _____

   _____

   _____

Continued on next page

4. _____ Fresh pear halves

    _____ Canned pear halves

    Why are the pear halves you checked most healthful?

    _____

    _____

    _____

5. _____ Fresh apple

    _____ Freshly-made applesauce

    Why is the apple you checked most healthful?

    _____

    _____

    _____

6. _____ Overripe banana

    _____ Underripe banana

    Why is the banana you checked most healthful?

    _____

    _____

    _____

Name _____ **Date** _____ **Class Hour**_____

CHAPTER 26 Fruits   **Text Pages 172-179**

   Consumer Power

Directions: Assume you are shopping for the following fruit. To get the most for your money, you must shop carefully. Figure the cost per ounce or unit for each fruit product and write it in the blank provided. Then circle the best buy for each fruit.

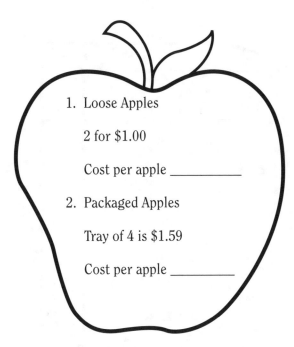

1. Loose Apples

    2 for $1.00

    Cost per apple _____

2. Packaged Apples

    Tray of 4 is $1.59

    Cost per apple _____

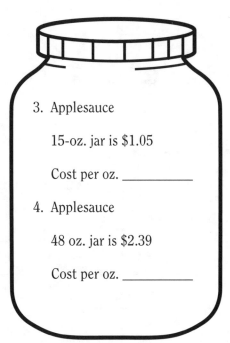

3. Applesauce

    15-oz. jar is $1.05

    Cost per oz. _____

4. Applesauce

    48 oz. jar is $2.39

    Cost per oz. _____

Continued on next page

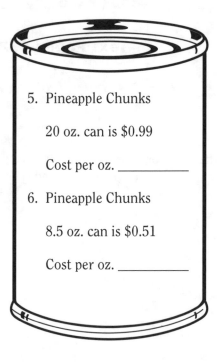

5. Pineapple Chunks

   20 oz. can is $0.99

   Cost per oz. _____

6. Pineapple Chunks

   8.5 oz. can is $0.51

   Cost per oz. _____

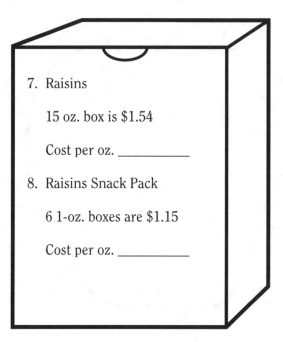

7. Raisins

   15 oz. box is $1.54

   Cost per oz. _____

8. Raisins Snack Pack

   6 1-oz. boxes are $1.15

   Cost per oz. _____

9. Sometimes the "best buy" is not the best choice for you. What factors beside price might you think about in buying fruit?

   _____

   _____

   _____

   _____

Study Guide

Completion: In the space to the left, write the word or words that **BEST** answer(s) each question.

_____ 1. How many servings from the Vegetable Group do you need each day for a healthful diet?

_____ 2. What vitamin is found in vegetables that are deep yellow, orange, or green?

_____ 3. What mineral is found in several vegetables?

_____ 4. What form of vegetable contains the most nutrients?

_____ 5. In what section of the supermarket are fresh vegetables found?

_____ 6. How should a good quality vegetable feel in relation to its size?

_____ 7. Where should most fresh vegetables be stored at home?

_____ 8. Name a vegetable that should be stored in a cool, dry place.

_____ 9. How long will fresh vegetables keep their quality?

_____ 10. How long do canned vegetables generally have to be cooked?

_____ 11. What will vegetables lose if they are soaked in water?

_____ 12. In what type of container should cut vegetables be stored?

_____ 13. To what texture should fresh vegetables be cooked?

_____ 14. What kind of flavor should cooked vegetables have?

_____ 15. What happens to nutrients when vegetables are overcooked?

_____ 16. What kind of texture do overcooked vegetables have?

_____ 17. How much water should be used in simmering frozen vegetables?

_____ 18. Why should baking soda not be added to cooked vegetables?

_____ 19. What kind of vegetables should not be heated in a microwave?

Continued on next page

Short Answer: Answer the following questions on the lines provided.

20. List the six parts of vegetable plants that supply vegetables and name one vegetable for each part.

_____

_____

_____

21. When can locally grown fresh vegetables be bought? What are two advantages of locally grown products?

_____

_____

22. List at least four ways vegetables can be used in the daily diet.

_____

_____

23. Describe the steps in preparing a raw carrot for a snack.

_____

_____

24. Why is it important to keep cut fresh vegetables crisp and fresh?

_____

_____

25. How does cooking affect vegetables?

_____

_____

26. Why are deep-fried vegetables less healthful than simmered or microwaved vegetables?

_____

27. Why should vegetables be cooked in a pan with a tight-fitting cover?

_____

28. Why should vegetables be served with their cooking liquid?

_____

Discovering Food and Nutrition Student Workbook Protected by Copyright ©

Name _____ **Date** _____ **Class Hour** _____

CHAPTER **27** Vegetables

Text Pages 180-187

   ## Find the Veggies

Directions: Ten different vegetables are hidden in the puzzle below. They are printed forwards, backwards, horizontally, and vertically. Circle each vegetable. Decide whether it is a good source of vitamin A, vitamin C, or calcium (it may be a good source of more than one) and list it under the appropriate nutrient(s).

S	E	O	T	A	T	O	P	T	E	E	W	S
T	O	M	A	S	U	O	U	C	A	S	S	R
O	S	T	E	L	R	U	M	O	K	A	L	E
R	E	S	W	E	N	A	P	P	E	R	S	P
R	O	T	W	E	I	P	K	S	L	O	S	P
A	T	A	O	E	P	O	I	A	M	N	E	E
C	A	B	B	A	G	E	N	O	T	R	O	P
T	M	B	R	B	R	O	C	C	O	L	I	N
R	O	A	O	R	E	S	W	E	T	E	N	E
E	T	G	C	O	E	L	E	A	K	A	N	E
M	O	S	K	A	N	N	W	P	T	R	S	R
S	P	I	N	O	S	P	I	N	A	C	H	G

Vitamin A	**Vitamin C**	**Calcium**
_____	_____	_____
_____	_____	_____
_____	_____	_____
_____	_____	_____
_____	_____	_____

Name _____ **Date** _____ **Class Hour** _____

▼ ▼ ▼ Steps to a Perfect Vegetable Tray

Directions: Tony is buying fresh vegetables to make a vegetable tray for a party. Follow Tony's steps from the supermarket and at home. Answer the questions about how Tony should choose, store, and prepare the vegetables on the lines below.

1. What qualities should Tony look for in picking out the vegetables?

   _____

   _____

   _____

   _____

2. When Tony gets home, how should he store the vegetables?

   _____

   _____

   _____

   _____

3. On the big day, how should Tony prepare the vegetables for the tray?

   _____

   _____

   _____

   _____

4. How should Tony store the prepared vegetables to keep them crisp until it is time for the party?

   _____

   _____

   _____

   _____

Discovering Food and Nutrition Student Workbook Protected by Copyright ©

Study Guide

Completion: In the space to the left, write the word or words that **BEST** complete(s) each statement.

_____ 1. Seeds that grow in a pod are called ___?___.

_____ 2. The sprouting plant stores ___?___ for itself in its seeds.

_____ 3. Legumes should be eaten with ___?___ for complete protein.

_____ 4. The ___?___ found in legumes helps strengthen the blood.

_____ 5. Legumes contain phosphorus and ___?___ to build strong bones and teeth.

_____ 6. Yellow or green legumes often used in soups are ___?___.

_____ 7. ___?___ are large red legumes with a hearty flavor.

_____ 8. One advantage of canned legumes is that they are ___?___.

_____ 9. Canned beans are not a good choice for someone on a low ___?___ diet.

_____ 10. Use a(n) ___?___ container to store uncooked legumes.

_____ 11. Tofu is made from ___?___.

_____ 12. Tofu is a good source of protein and ___?___.

_____ 13. You get 2 1/4 to 3 cups (550 to 750 mL) of cooked beans from ___?___ of dry beans.

_____ 14. When soaking 1 cup (250 mL) of dry beans, use ___?___ of water.

_____ 15. Most legumes need ___?___ hours of simmering to become tender.

_____ 16. Beans that fall apart and are mushy are ___?___.

_____ 17. When cooking 1 cup (250 mL) of dry beans, use ___?___ of water.

_____ 18. Beans should be simmered with the cover off the pot ___?___.

_____ 19. Dry beans to be used in casseroles and soups should be ___?___.

Continued on next page

_____ 20. Beans are ___?___ when tomatoes and sugar are added at the beginning.

_____ 21. Adding baking soda to dry beans while they are cooking destroys ___?___.

Short Answer: Answer the following questions on the lines provided.

22. Name at least six nutrients that are found in legumes.

_____

_____

_____

23. Compare the cost of protein from meat and legumes. Can legumes be used to substitute for meat on an equal nutritional basis? Why?

_____

_____

_____

24. Why do older dried legumes need longer to cook than fresher ones?

_____

_____

_____

25. How should leftover cooked legumes be stored for a few days? For two weeks?

_____

_____

_____

26. Give three suggestions for using canned legumes in the daily diet.

_____

_____

_____

27. What are two time-saving uses of the microwave in legume cookery?

_____

_____

CHAPTER 28 Legumes   **Text Pages 188-195**

   Legume Magic Square

Directions: Find the term that best fits each description. Write the number of the correct term in the small box in the appropriate lettered space. If all your answers are correct, the total of the numbers, or the "magic number" will be the same in each row across and down. Write the magic number in the space provided.

Terms

1. legumes

2. simmered

3. swell

4. tomatoes

5. B vitamins

6. incomplete

7. tofu

8. iron

9. soaking

10. calcium

11. boiled

12. baking soda

A	B	C
D	E	F
G	H	I

The Magic Number is _____.

Descriptions

A. Seeds that grow in a pod.
B. The kind of protein found in legumes.
C. A nutrient found in legumes that strengthens blood.
D. A nutrient found in legumes needed for growth and health.
E. A custard-like product made from soybeans.
F. What legumes do when cooked.
G. What most dry legumes need before cooking.
H. How legumes should be cooked.
I. This ingredient will toughen beans.

Name _____ Date _____ Class Hour_____

CHAPTER **28** Legumes   **Text Pages 188-195**

   Legume Calculations

Directions: Fill in the chart by calculating price per ounce of the legumes listed below. Then answer the questions on the lines provided.

Legume	Processing	Size	Cost	Unit Cost
Great Northern Beans	Dried	2 lb. (9089 g)	$0.86	1. _____
Great Northern Beans	Canned	15 oz. (425 g)	$0.51	2. _____
Kidney Beans	Dried	1 lb. (454 g)	$0.68	3. _____
Kidney Beans	Canned	15 oz. (425 g)	$0.56	4. _____

5. Is it accurate to directly compare unit prices of dried and canned beans? Explain.

_____

_____

_____

6. Most of the canned beans are about the same price. How would you decide which to buy?

_____

_____

7. What are the advantages of buying dried legumes?

_____

_____

8. What are the advantages of buying canned legumes?

_____

_____

Discovering Food and Nutrition Student Workbook Protected by Copyright ©

Study Guide

Completion: In the space to the left, write the word or words that **BEST** complete(s) each statement.

_____   1. Poultry contains less ___?___ if the skin is removed.

_____   2. The ___?___ affects the amount of fat a serving of poultry contains.

_____   3. The amount of ___?___ is about the same in poultry and meat.

_____   4. The meat of turkeys has a ___?___ flavor than that of chickens.

_____   5. Uncooked chicken can be sold whole or cut in ___?___, ___?___, or
_____   ___?___.

_____

_____   6. Before deciding what form of poultry to buy, consider ___?___ and
_____   ___?___.

_____   7. A(n) ___?___ is the most common type of fresh or frozen chicken sold.

_____   8. Poultry that is ___?___ can be broiled or roasted.

_____   9. There should be no ___?___ on good quality fresh poultry.

_____   10. Poultry that contains bones provides ___?___ servings per pound.

_____   11. Boneless poultry provides ___?___ servings per pound.

_____   12. Fresh poultry should be stored in ___?___ of the refrigerator.

_____   13. A harmful bacteria called ___?___ can be found in raw poultry.

_____   14. To keep bacteria from spreading , wash ___?___, ___?___, and ___?___
                               carefully.

_____

_____

_____   15. ___?___ cooked poultry is tender, moist, and flavorful.

Continued on next page

_____ 16. When poultry reaches an internal temperature of ___?___, it is done.

_____ 17. The juices of fully cooked poultry are ___?___.

_____ 18. Place the meatier parts toward the ___?___ of the microwave dish.

_____ 19. Fat and juices ___?___ microwave cooking time of poultry.

Short Answer: Answer the following questions on the lines provided.

20. Why is poultry considered a nutritious food?

_____

_____

_____

_____

21. Why shouldn't cost per pound be compared when buying poultry? What should be compared instead?

_____

_____

_____

22. What is the formula for figuring cost per serving?

_____

_____

23. How should frozen poultry be thawed?

_____

24. Why should a stuffed bird not be refrigerated overnight before roasting?

_____

25. Why is frying a less healthful way of preparing chicken than roasting or braising?

_____

26. Why should poultry skin be pierced before the pieces are microwaved?

_____

CHAPTER 29 Poultry   **Text Pages 196-205**

Telephone Terms

Directions: The numbers beneath the answer blanks below correspond to the numbers of a telephone's buttons. There are three letters on each button (except for the buttons marked 1 and 0). Decide which of the three letters on the indicated button is used in the answer. Write the correct letters in the spaces. If you decide on an answer from the clue alone, use the numbers to check your accuracy.

1. Birds raised for food.

    ___ ___ ___ ___ ___ ___ ___
     7   6   8   5   8   7   9

2. A mineral found in chicken or turkey.

    ___ ___ ___ ___ ___ ___ ___ ___ ___ ___
     7   4   6   7   7   4   6   7   8   7

3. A cooking method that adds fat to poultry.

    ___ ___ ___ ___ ___ ___
     3   7   9   4   6   4

4. Most common type of chicken sold.

    ___ ___ ___ ___ ___ ___ ___
     2   7   6   4   5   3   7

5. The meatiest kind of poultry.

    ___ ___ ___ ___ ___ ___
     4   7   2   3   3   2

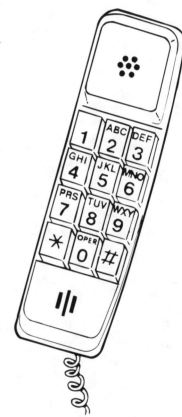

6. The cost per pound for poultry.

    ___ ___ ___ ___ ___ ___ ___ ___
     8   6   4   8   2   6   7   8

7. An example of a cured poultry product.

    ___ ___ ___ ___ ___ ___ ___ ___ ___ ___ ___
     3   7   2   6   5   3   8   7   8   3   7

8. A harmful bacteria often found in poultry.

    ___ ___ ___ ___ ___ ___ ___ ___ ___ ___
     7   2   5   6   6   6   3   5   5   2

9. A method of cooking poultry in liquid.

    ___ ___ ___ ___ ___ ___ ___ ___
     2   7   2   4   7   4   6   4

CHAPTER 29 Poultry   **Text Pages 196-205**

▼ ▼ ▼ Poultry Math

Directions: Read the situations below and write your calculations in the box under each situation. Write your answers on the lines provided on the righthand side of each box.

1. Jan wants to buy 3 pounds (1500 g) chicken thighs for $1.29 per pound. How much will she pay? How many servings will the thighs provide?

_____

2. Don is buying turkey cutlets for $2.69 per pound. The package weighs 4 pounds, 8 ounces (2227 g). How much will the cutlets cost?

_____

3. Allen bought a 2 pound (1000 g) fryer for $1.19 a pound. How many servings will the fryer make? What will his cost per serving be?

_____

4. Darin is having 12 people at his house for a family dinner. He wants to roast a turkey. How big a turkey would he need to serve everyone? He'd also like to buy 2 pounds (1000 g) extra for turkey sandwiches. If turkey costs $1.19 per pound, how much would a turkey big enough for dinner and sandwiches cost?

_____

CHAPTER 30 **Fish and Shellfish**   **Text Pages 206-215**

Study Guide

Completion: In the space to the left, write the word or words that **BEST** complete(s) each statement.

_____ 1. Cod and haddock are kinds of ___?___.

_____ 2. Crabs and oysters are kinds of ___?___.

_____ 3. Fish and shellfish are good sources of ___?___ protein.

_____ 4. Saltwater fish are a good source of the mineral ___?___.

_____ 5. A good source of ___?___ is canned salmon, eaten with its bones.

_____ 6. Most of the fat found in fish is ___?___.

_____ 7. When the entire fish as it is caught is sold, it is called ___?___.

_____ 8. A fish whose insides have been removed is called a ___?___ fish.

_____ 9. A ___?___ fish has had scales, insides, head, tail, and fins removed.

_____ 10. Slices cut across a large fish are called ___?___.

_____ 11. ___?___ are sides of fish cut away from the ribs and backbone.

_____ 12. To get a 3 oz. (84 g) serving of cooked fish without bones takes ___?___ of whole or drawn fish.

_____ 13. One pound (500 g) of fish steaks will provide ___?___ servings.

_____ 14. The highest grade of fish is ___?___.

_____ 15. Fresh fish can be kept ___?___ in the coldest part of the refrigerator.

_____ 16. Cooked fish should be stored in ___?___ in the refrigerator.

_____ 17. ___?___ is used to make imitation shellfish products.

_____ 18. Fresh shellfish should be used within ___?___.

_____ 19. Cooked shellfish can be refrigerated for ___?___ days.

Continued on next page

_____ 20. Fish is naturally tender because it has little ___?___.

_____ 21. When cooked fish is tested with a fork, it should ___?___ easily.

_____ 22. To microwave fish, use 100% power for ___?___ per pound (500 g).

Short Answer: Answer the following questions on the lines provided.

23. Explain the differences between fish and shellfish.

_____

_____

24. Describe the signs of quality to look for in buying whole fresh fish.

_____

_____

_____

25. Describe how to buy and store fresh shellfish.

_____

_____

_____

26. Describe how to thaw frozen fish.

_____

27. Describe the color change fish undergoes when it is cooked.

_____

28. Explain how to use the 10-minute rule for cooking fish.

_____

_____

29. How should you keep fish from drying out when broiling and microwaving it?

_____

_____

CHAPTER 30 Fish and Shellfish   **Text Pages 206-215**

Fishy Calculating

Directions: Read the problems below and calculate the answers to each question. In the blank to the left of the question, write the letter of the fish that contains the answer to the problem.

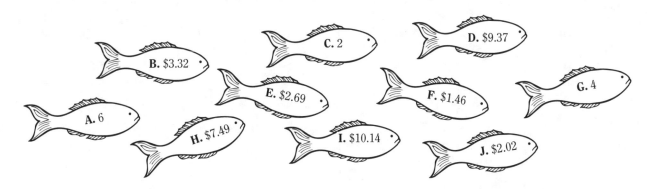

_____   1. Jason bought cod fillets for dinner. The cod cost $4.99 per pound and had a net weight of 1 lb. 8 oz. (750 g). How much did Jason pay for the fish?

_____   2. The fresh red snapper fillets Marnie was looking at cost $4.39 per pound. If she bought 3 pounds (1500 g), how much would the fillets cost per serving?

_____   3. Andy needs 24 oz. (750 g) of tuna for a casserole. The 6 oz. (170 g) cans cost $0.83 and the 12 oz. (340 g) cans cost $2.09. What would he pay if he buys the most economical size?

_____   4. Michelle caught a 4 lb. (2000 g) trout on a fishing trip. How many servings will the fish provide?

_____   5. Dan bought 2 pounds of pollock at $2.99 per pound and a can of red salmon for $3.39. How much was his total bill?

_____   6. Lou bought 2 pounds of salmon steaks at $4.99 per pound. How many servings will the steaks make?

_____   7. Amy bought a package of frozen perch for $3.49, and a l lb. (500 g) of orange roughy for $4.49. She gave the grocery clerk $10.00. How much change did she get back?

Name _____ **Date** _____ **Class Hour** _____

CHAPTER **30** Fish and Shellfish   **Text Pages 206-215**

Hidden Fish and Shellfish

Directions: Hidden in the puzzle below are the names of 18 fish and shellfish. They are printed forwards, backwards, horizontally, and vertically. Circle the names and decide if each is a fish or a shellfish. Write each name on the appropriate list below.

```
U   S   C   A   L   L   O   P   S   R   M
H   A   L   S   F   T   R   O   U   T   T
C   R   A   B   A   C   I   L   G   S   U
R   D   M   E   N   O   M   L   A   S   B
E   I   S   T   U   D   U   O   K   A   I
P   N   B   A   T   P   S   C   C   B   L
M   E   Q   U   A   L   S   K   O   I   A
I   S   A   L   L   M   E   D   D   C   H
R   E   T   S   B   O   L   Y   D   W   P
H   C   A   T   F   I   S   H   A   T   E
S   R   E   T   S   Y   O   V   H   S   I
```

FISH		**SHELLFISH**	
_____	_____	_____	_____
_____	_____	_____	_____
_____	_____	_____	_____
_____	_____	_____	_____
_____	_____	_____	_____
_____	_____	_____	_____

Study Guide

Completion: In the space to the left, write the word or words that **BEST** complete(s) each statement.

_____ 1. Meat is a good source of the nutrients___?___, ___?___, and ___?___.

_____

_____

_____ 2. A serving of cooked meat is ___?___ ounces (g).

_____ 3. Meat varies in fat so choose ___?___ meat for low-fat eating.

_____ 4. Before you cook meat, you should ___?___ the fat.

_____ 5. Consider ___?___, ___?___, and ___?___ when buying meat.

_____

_____

_____ 6. The pink or reddish part of meat is the lean or ___?___.

_____ 7. Flecks of fat throughout the meat are called ___?___.

_____ 8. Surrounding the muscle is tough ___?___ tissue.

_____ 9. A portion of meat from a specific part of the animal is a ___?___ of meat.

_____ 10. The large sections of meat into which animals are divided are ___?___.

_____ 11. The smaller pieces of meat sold at the supermarket are called ___?___.

_____ 12. The top grade of meat is ___?___.

_____ 13. The least expensive of the three top grades of beef is ___?___.

_____ 14. The amount of ___?___ and ___?___ affects the number of servings per pound.

_____

_____ 15. The cuts of meat that usually cost less are the ___?___ cuts.

Continued on next page

_____ 16. Cook meat to at least ___?___ to insure that it is safe to eat.

_____ 17. Tender cuts of meat like beef loin and pork can be cooked by ___?___ heat.

_____ 18. Meats with more connective tissue must be ___?___ during preparation or cooking.

_____ 19. An illness caused by undercooked pork is ___?___.

Short Answer: Answer the following questions on the lines provided.

20. Why is planning needed to include meat in a low-fat diet?

_____

_____

21. Why are some cooking methods more suitable for a low-fat eating plan?

_____

_____

22. Describe how fresh meat should be stored when brought home from the supermarket. How soon should it be used?

_____

_____

_____

23. Compare and contrast the following methods of cooking meat: roasting; broiling; panbroiling; braising.

_____

_____

_____

_____

24. List at least three suggestions for successfully microwaving meat?

_____

_____

_____

How Much Does a Serving Cost?

Directions: Listed below are several cuts of meat and their cost per pound. Also given are the number of servings the meat provides per pound. Figure the cost per serving for each meat and answer the question below on the lines provided.

Cut of Meat	Cost Per Pound	Servings per Pound	Cost per Serving
Beef			
Ground Beef (lean)	$1.89	4	1._____
Ground Beef (regular)	$1.39	4	2._____
Sirloin Steak	$3.29	4	3._____
Bottom Round Roast	$1.99	3	4._____
Lamb			
Loin Chop	$6.29	3	5._____
Shoulder Roast	$2.99	3	6._____
Leg of Lamb Steak	$3.79	3	7._____
Pork			
Bacon	$2.39	4	8._____
Ham (boneless)	$4.29	4	9._____
Loin Chop	$2.49	3	10._____

11. What was the most expensive meat per pound? _____

12. Why do you think this cut was most expensive? _____

_____

13. What was the least expensive meat per pound?_____

14. Why do you think this cut was least expensive? _____

_____

_____

15. What conclusions can you draw from this activity? _____

_____

_____

CHAPTER 31 Meat   **Text Pages 216-227**

 Meat Puzzler

Directions: When your food budget is limited and meat is expensive, what can you do? To discover one solution to this problem, write the word or phrase for each definition in the blanks to the left. Transfer the circled letter to the appropriate blank at the bottom.

1. __ Ⓞ __ __ __   Ham is an example of this kind of meat.

2. Ⓞ __ __ __   Use this at the end when broiling meat.

3. __ __ Ⓞ __   Meat that comes from mature cattle over one year old.

4. __ __ __ __ Ⓞ __ __ __   A cooking method that can be used with tender cuts of meat.

5. __ Ⓞ __ __ __ __   What cooking makes meat.

6. Ⓞ __ __ __ __ __   A grade that has less fat than other grades.

7. __ __ __ __ Ⓞ __ __ __   This cooking method can be used with less-tender cuts of meat.

8. __ __ __ __ __ __ __ __ __ Ⓞ __ __   Used to find the internal temperature of cooked meat.

9. __ __ __ __ Ⓞ   Grade of beef that is most expensive.

10. __ __ __ Ⓞ   Meat is a good source of this nutrient.

11. __ __ __ __ __ __ Ⓞ __   A mixture of acid and seasonings that flavors and tenderizes meat.

12. __ __ Ⓞ __ __   Juices of this color indicate meat is done.

13. __ __ Ⓞ __ __ __ __ __   Flecks of fat found throughout the muscle.

14. Ⓞ __ __ __ __ __ __ __ __ __ __   Tough tissue that surrounds the sections of muscle.

Continued on next page

Meat Puzzler

15. __ Ⓞ __ __ __ __   The lean, red or pinkish part of meat.

16. __ __ Ⓞ __ __ __   Kind of cuts sold in a supermarket.

17. __ __ __ Ⓞ __ __ __ __   A cooking method used with large tender cuts of meat.

__ __ __   __ __ __ __   __ __ __ __ __ __   __ __ __ __
1 2 3   4 5 6 7   8 9 10 11 12 13   14 15 16 17

LOOK at the Label

Directions: Shown below is a label from a package of meat. Read the label and answer the questions on the lines provided.

1. What kind of meat is in this package? _____

2. How much does this meat cost per pound?_____

3. How much does the meat in this package weigh?_____

4. What is the price of this package of meat? _____

5. What does the date on the label mean? _____

   _____

6. What is the retail cut of this meat? _____

7. What grade is this meat? _____

8. Is this a tender or a less-tender cut of meat? _____

9. What are two ways you could cook this piece of meat?

   _____

   _____

10. How many servings could you get from this package of meat? _____

   _____

Study Guide

Completion: In the space to the left, write the word or words that **BEST** complete(s) each statement.

_____ 1. Eggs are a bargain because they are low in ___?___.

_____ 2. Fat and cholesterol are contained in the egg ___?___.

_____ 3. A limit of ___?___ eggs a week is suggested by health experts.

_____ 4. High quality eggs are graded ___?___ or ___?___.

_____

_____ 5. Eggs should be refrigerated in ___?___.

_____ 6. Eggs should be used within ___?___ weeks.

_____ 7. ___?___, a bacteria sometimes found in raw eggs, may cause food poisoning.

_____ 8. To prevent food poisoning, ___?___ all eggs you eat.

_____ 9. Eggs used in custard help ___?___ the ingredients.

_____ 10. When egg whites are beaten, they trap ___?___ for lightness.

_____ 11. When eggs are ___?___, they separate more easily.

_____ 12. If egg whites contain any ___?___ from the egg yolk, they will not beat.

_____ 13. ___?___ temperature gives the best volume when beating egg whites.

_____ 14. Beaten egg whites that are thick, white, and shiny are in the ___?___ stage.

_____ 15. When egg whites are overbeaten, they are ___?___ and break into pieces.

_____ 16. A mixture of beaten egg whites and sugar is called a ___?___.

_____ 17. Eggs should be cooked at ___?___ or medium temperatures.

_____ 18. Whole eggs can explode in the microwave because of built up ___?___ and ___?___.

_____

Continued on next page

_____ 19. Pierce the egg ___?___ to let steam escape when microwaving eggs.

_____ 20. The egg ___?___ cooks fastest in the microwave.

Short Answer: Answer the following questions on the lines provided.

21. Describe how to break an egg.

_____

_____

_____

22. Why shouldn't you break an egg directly into other ingredients?

_____

_____

23. Describe how to separate an egg.

_____

_____

_____

24. Describe undercooked, properly cooked, and overcooked eggs.

_____

_____

_____

25. How are poached eggs and eggs cooked in the shell similar and different?

_____

_____

_____

26. How are scrambled eggs and omelets similar and different?

_____

_____

_____

CHAPTER 32 Eggs   Text Pages 228-235

Buying Eggs

Directions: Answer the following questions on the lines provided.

1. Sam is buying eggs for baking a cake and some cookies. Large eggs cost 92 cents a dozen while small eggs are 79 cents a dozen. Which size eggs should he buy? Why?

_____

_____

2. Carrie is looking at eggs in the supermarket. The store is having a sale on eggs and has extra cartons of eggs sitting in the aisle beside the refrigerated egg case. Does it matter if Carrie takes her carton from the aisle display or the refrigerator case? Why?

_____

_____

_____

3. Diane is buying eggs for her families' use. The large eggs cost 99 cents a dozen while the medium eggs cost 90 cents. Which eggs are of better quality? Why?

_____

_____

4. Brad's store has brown eggs and white eggs at the same price. Brad wants to buy the most nutritious and best quality eggs. Which should he buy?

_____

_____

5. The supermarket where Linda is shopping has cracked eggs for 1/2 price. Should she buy them? Why?

_____

_____

_____

Name _____ **Date** _____ **Class Hour** _____

CHAPTER 32 Eggs

Text Pages 228-235

   ## The Key to Egg Cookery

Directions: To find the key to successful egg cookery, fill in the blanks to answer each question. The number of spaces indicates the number of letters in the word. If you answer the questions correctly, you will be able to unscramble the circled letters to find the key to egg cookery.

1. What is a mixture of egg whites and sugar beaten into stiff peaks?

   ◯ _ _ _ _ _ ◯ _ _

2. What gets trapped in egg whites when they are beaten?

   _ _ ◯ _ _ _ _ _ ◯ _ _

3. What causes whole eggs to explode when cooked in the microwave?

   _ _ ◯ _ _ _

   ◯ _ _ _ _ _ _ _

4. When egg whites are beaten, what is the stage where the whites are transparent and bubbles form?

   _ _ ◯ _ _ _

5. What ingredient can be used with eggs to prepare omelets?

   ◯ _ _ ◯ _

6. When egg whites are beaten, what is the stage where they stand up in peaks that bend over?

   _ _ _ _ ◯ _ _ ◯ _ _ _

7. What is the name of eggs that are gently stirred into soft curds during cooking?

   ◯ _ ◯ _ _ _ _ _ _ _

8. What is the substance in egg yolks that leads some people to avoid eating eggs?

   _ _ ◯ _ _ _ ◯ _ _ _ _

9. The key to egg cookery is:

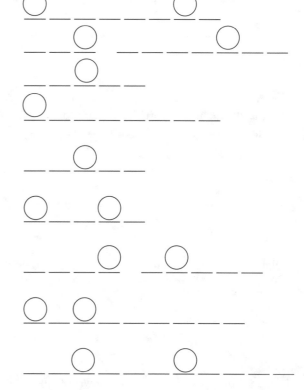

_ _ _ _ _ _ _ _ _ _ _ _ _ _

Name _____ Date _____ Class Hour_____

CHAPTER 33 Salads   **Text Pages 236-241**

Study Guide

Completion: In the space at the left, write the word or words that **BEST** complete(s) each statement.

_____ 1. The greens, vegetables, and fruits used in making salads are good sources of ___?___ and ___?___.

_____

_____ 2. Using whole grains and cooked beans in salads provide ___?___ and ___?___.

_____

_____ 3. Using meat, cheese, and eggs in salads provides ___?___.

_____ 4. Foods that are high in ___?___ and ___?___, like eggs, should be used sparingly in salads.

_____

_____ 5. Salad greens should be stored in ___?___ in the refrigerator.

_____ 6. The ___?___ should be removed from iceberg lettuce before it is stored.

_____ 7. Tiny plants just starting to grow from seeds are called ___?___.

_____ 8. The prepared salad dressings that are more healthful are low in ___?___, ___?___, and ___?___.

_____

_____ 9. Most salad dressings, after they are made or opened, should be stored ___?___.

_____ 10. Three ways salads can be put together are ___?___, ___?___, and ___?___.

_____

_____

_____ 11. Gelatin is often used in making ___?___ salads.

_____ 12. The dressing will be thinned if ___?___ is left on ingredients used to make a tossed salad.

_____ 13. Greens for a tossed salad should be in ___?___ pieces.

Continued on next page

_____ 14. Greens that are cut with a knife quickly get ___?___.

_____ 15. A tossed salad that won't be used right away should be ___?___ and ___?___ so it stays fresh and crisp.

_____

_____ 16. The dressing should be added to a tossed salad ___?___.

_____ 17. If dressing is added too far ahead of time, greens will ___?___.

_____ 18. Seasoned, toasted bread cubes are called ___?___.

_____ 19. The ___?___ is the foundation of an arranged salad.

_____ 20. The main part of an arranged salad is the ___?___.

Short Answer: Answer the following questions on the lines provided.

21. What are four different ways salads can be used as part of a menu?

_____

_____

22. What are two types of sprouts commonly used in salads? How should they be stored?

_____

_____

_____

23. What two purposes does dressing serve in a salad?

_____

_____

24. What is the special characteristic of a molded salad?

_____

_____

_____

25. What would be the advantage of having a "mini salad bar" in your refrigerator?

_____

_____

CHAPTER 33 Salads   **Text Pages 236-241**

 A Tossed Salad

Directions: Sixteen ingredients for a salad have been "tossed" into the hidden word puzzle below. The ingredients are printed forwards, backwards, horizontally, and vertically. Circle each ingredient and list it under the appropriate heading below.

```
A  S  D  E  E  S  R  E  W  O  L  F  N  U  S  M  G  I
Y  N  L  R  E  X  O  N  I  F  T  Q  U  H  R  P  R  C
S  I  D  S  C  J  M  C  A  R  R  O  T  S  E  N  E  K
P  S  J  L  U  Y  A  R  A  G  E  N  I  V  B  R  E  H
I  I  W  C  T  T  I  W  E  A  V  K  M  R  M  O  N  E
N  A  B  H  T  O  N  Q  I  T  B  N  G  A  U  W  P  S
A  R  I  C  E  B  E  R  G  L  E  T  T  U  C  E  E  C
C  L  U  V  L  O  N  I  O  N  S  H  C  G  U  R  P  A
H  O  W  M  F  D  E  S  N  O  T  U  O  R  C  A  P  R
N  O  N  F  A  T  Y  O  G  U  R  T  T  M  A  I  E  O
Y  A  L  N  E  C  I  U  J  N  O  M  E  L  T  K  R  L
K  C  S  A  L  F  A  L  F  A  S  P  R  O  U  T  S  E
```

Greens	Vegetables	Toppings	Dressing
_____	_____	_____	_____
_____	_____	_____	_____
_____	_____	_____	_____
_____	_____	_____	_____
_____	_____	_____	_____

Mystery Salad

Directions: To solve the puzzle, read each clue. Write the word or words that fit the clue in the corresponding line of the puzzle, one letter in each box. When all the boxes are filled, the name of the mystery salad will be spelled out in the darker squares.

1.

2.

3.

4.

5.

6.

7.

Clues

1. Where salad greens should be stored.

2. The foundation of an arranged salad.

3. A kind of sprouts used in green salads.

4. In this kind of salad, the ingredients form an attractive pattern.

5. A common kind of salad green.

6. A salad ingredient that helps hold the mixture together.

7. This type of salad often contains meat and/or pasta.

The mystery salad is: _____

CHAPTER 34 Soups   **Text Pages 242-247**

Study Guide

Completion: In the space to the left, write the word or words that **BEST** complete(s) each statement.

_____ 1. A ___?___ is a thick soup made with vegetables, fish, or seafood.

_____ 2. Soup is as nutritious as the ___?___ in it.

_____ 3. Water-soluble vitamins and minerals are present in the liquid called ___?___.

_____ 4. Adding meat to soups provides ___?___, increasing the nutritional value.

_____ 5. When soups are chilled, the ___?___ rises and hardens.

_____ 6. ___?___ or ___?___ soups are convenient because they can be prepared by heating or by adding water or milk and heating.

_____

_____ 7. One drawback of convenience soups is that they are high in ___?___.

_____ 8. Canned and packaged soups should be stored in a(n) ___?___.

_____ 9. Cooked soups can be stored in the refrigerator for ___?___ days.

_____ 10. Soup can be made from scratch by cooking bony pieces of meat or poultry in ___?___ with seasonings.

_____ 11. ___?___, which is a flavorful broth, requires long, slow cooking.

_____ 12. Add ingredients to convenience soups to provide more ___?___ and ___?___.

_____

_____ 13. Cream soups are often prepared from a ___?___ base.

_____ 14. Two bases for easy homemade soup are ___?___ or ___?___.

_____

_____ 15. Fresh vegetables that require longer cooking time may be precooked by ___?___ in oil.

Continued on next page

_____ 16. Herbs and spices are used to ___?___ soup.

_____ 17. Grains or pureed cooked dry beans may be used to ___?___ soup.

_____ 18. When microwaving soup, bring it to a temperature of ___?___.

_____ 19. Stir soup heated in the microwave once or twice so it will ___?___.

Short Answer: Answer the following questions on the lines provided.

20. Name at least three ways soup can be used when planning menus.

_____

_____

_____

21. Discuss at least three reasons why soup can be nutritious.

_____

_____

_____

22. Describe two ways to make soups more healthful.

_____

_____

23. List two suggestions for making convenience soups more flavorful and nutritious.

_____

_____

24. Describe two techniques used to thicken soup.

_____

_____

25. What type of container should you use for microwaving soup?

_____

_____

_____

CHAPTER 34 Soups

Soup Savvy

Directions: Assume you are a food columnist named Antonio. The topic for your column today is Soup Savvy. You have received the letters below. Answer the letters on the lines provided.

1. Dear Antonio,

   I made some creamy vegetable soup with a white sauce and cooked carrots, celery, and potatoes. However, the soup curdled long before the vegetables were tender. What should I have done?

                                                         Signed,
                                                         Curdled on Soup

   _____

   _____

   _____

2. Dear Antonio,

   I don't like to drink milk but I love cream soups like cream of broccoli, cream of potato, and clam chowder. Can I count the milk in these soups toward the number of servings of milk I need each day?

                                                         Signed,
                                                         Avoids Milk

   _____

   _____

   _____

3. Dear Antonio,

   I eat a lot of soup because it is fast and convenient and I like it. How healthful is soup? Are there ways to make it more healthful for me?

                                                         Signed,
                                                         Wants to be Healthy

   _____

   _____

   _____

CHAPTER 34 Soups

   ## Soup Match Ups

Directions: Match each definition in the left column with the correct term from the right column. Write the letter of the term in the space provided. Do not use any term more than once. Some terms will not be used.

Definitions

_____ 1. Soup that only needs to be heated and served.

_____ 2. A thick soup made with vegetables, fish, or seafood.

_____ 3. A flavorful liquid made by long slow cooking of meat or poultry in water.

_____ 4. A soup made from cooked vegetables, meat, or poultry.

_____ 5. A soup often based on white sauce.

_____ 6. A clear flavorful liquid that can be made from cubes or granules.

_____ 7. The liquid in soup.

Terms

A. Bouillon

B. Broth

C. Chowder

D. Convenience soup

E. Cream soup

F. Hearty soup

G. Light soup

H. Microwave soup

I. Stock

CHAPTER 35 One-Dish Meals   **Text Pages 248-255**

Study Guide

_____ 1. A ___?___ of meat is necessary for preparing one-dish meals.

_____ 2. Whole grains in one-dish meals are healthful because they provide ___?___.

_____ 3. Using convenience foods helps reduce the ___?___ of one-dish meals.

_____ 4. Canned fish and dried soup are examples of ___?___ used in one-dish meals.

_____ 5. Convenience foods are often less healthful and are high in ___?___ and ___?___.

_____

_____ 6. A one-dish meal cooked on top of the range may be called a ___?___ meal.

_____ 7. Cooking food quickly in a small amount of oil is known as ___?___.

_____ 8. A ___?___ is a large pan with a rounded bottom that is used for stir-frying.

_____ 9. The most abundant type of ingredient in a stir-fry recipe is ___?___.

_____ 10. Fish, poultry, meat, or tofu can be used to supply ___?___ in stir-fry.

_____ 11. Stir-fry mixtures are often served over ___?___.

_____ 12. Slicing or chopping the ___?___ before cooking is important when stir-frying.

_____ 13. ___?___ are not added to stir-fry until near the end of cooking.

_____ 14. Tough ingredients require ___?___ stir-frying time than tender ingredients.

_____ 15. A mixture of water and ___?___ is used to thicken stir-fry.

_____ 16. A ___?___ helps hold ingredients together and thicken a casserole.

_____ 17. English muffin halves or French bread slices can also be used as a pizza ___?___.

Continued on next page

_____ 18. Use the microwave to ___?___ or ___?___ meat or vegetables for one-dish meals.

_____

_____ 19. Chopped vegetables can be ___?___ in the microwave in oil.

Short Answer: Answer the following questions on the lines provided.

20. List two advantages of one-dish meals.

_____

21. What are some ingredients that help lower the fat content of one-dish meals?

_____

_____

22. Discuss the advantages and disadvantages of using convenience foods in one-dish meals.

_____

_____

23. How can cooks make their own "convenience" foods?

_____

_____

24. Why are foods cut into small pieces when stir-frying? Why are ingredients kept separate?

_____

_____

25. When making a stir-fry recipe, why are vegetables cut on a different cutting board than meat, poultry, or fish?

_____

_____

26. List the key ingredients in a casserole and tell the purpose each serves.

_____

_____

_____

CHAPTER 35 One-Dish Meals   **Text Pages 248-255**

   ## Scrambled Ingredients

Directions: Listed below in scrambled form are nine ingredients often used in one-dish meals. Unscramble the letters to discover the ingredient. On the lines provided, describe how each ingredient is used in a one-dish meal.

Scrambled Ingredients	Ingredients	Use in One-Dish Meals
1. vieencnoecn dosof	_____	_____
		_____
2. ohlwe risgan	_____	_____
		_____
3. ilo	_____	_____
		_____
4. lporuyt	_____	_____
		_____
5. ccahtrorsn	_____	_____
		_____
6. inrbde	_____	_____
		_____
7. snsoagnise	_____	_____
		_____
8. gpnipsot	_____	_____
		_____
9. tysae gdohu	_____	_____
		_____

CHAPTER 35 One-Dish Meals   **Text Pages 248-255**

   Crossword Puzzle

Directions: Fill in the crossword puzzle by placing the answers to each number below in the appropriate space.

Across
1. A food that can be used as a base for pizza. (2 words)
3. Serves as a binder in casseroles. (2 words)
8. A type of one-dish meal made on the range. (2 words)
9. A large pan with a rounded bottom used for stir-frying.
10. A food often served with stir-fry.
11. An ingredient mixed with water for thickening.
14. An ingredient in which stir-fry is cooked.
16. Pizza crust is usually made from this. (2 words)
17. One of the last ingredients to cook when stir-frying.
19. A type of one-dish meal with a crust or base, sauce, toppings, and cheese.
22. A topping for casseroles.
25. A mixture of foods baked together.
26. One-dish meals can be cooked on this appliance.
29. A common ingredient in stir-frying.
31. A type of protein convenience food used in one-dish meals. (2 words)
32. An important step in using ground beef in a casserole.
33. A kind of vegetable often used in stir-frying.
34. A nutrient often supplied by one-dish meals.

Down
1. Whole grains provide this in one-dish meals.
2. A type of pan often used to make pizza. (2 words)
4. An ingredient used as a liquid in casseroles.
5. Ingredients added to flavor one-dish meals.
6. Cooking food quickly in hot oil. (2 words)
7. An appliance used to thaw or precook ingredients before preparing one-dish meals.
11. May be used to reduce the preparation time of one-dish meals. (2 words)
12. A food used to complete a meal when serving a one-dish meal.
13. A topping used on pizza.
15. Protein food used to lower fat content in one-dish meals. (2 words)
18. A kind of cheese used on pizza.
19. Provides protein in one-dish meals.
20. A type of ingredient in casseroles that adds nutrients and flavor while helping the binder work.
21. A type of ingredient in casseroles that helps thicken them and hold ingredients together.
23. To cut ingredients into small pieces for stir-fry.
24. A one-dish meal similar to soup, but with less liquid.
27. A spice used to flavor some one-dish meals.
28. One of the first ingredients to cook when stir-frying.
30. What you do to cheese before it is put on pizza.

Continued on next page

Crossword Puzzle

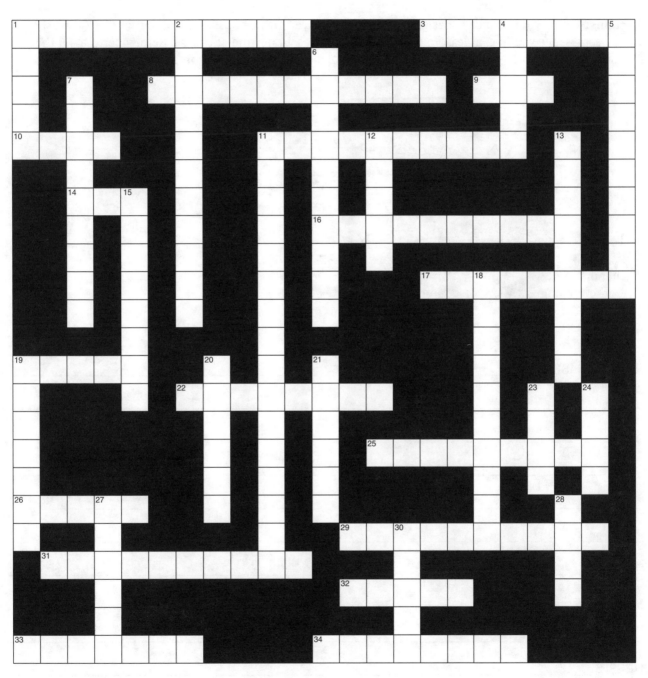

Designer Pizza

Directions: This is your chance to design a pizza that suits your taste buds! Start out by choosing a crust or base. Select a sauce you like, at least four toppings, and at least one kind of cheese. Remember that all the ingredients should work together to create a pleasing blend of flavors and textures.

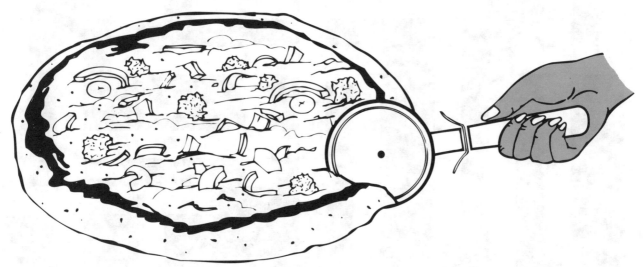

CRUST OR BASE:_____

_____

_____

SAUCE:_____

_____

_____

TOPPINGS:_____

_____

_____

CHEESE: _____

_____

Study Guide

Completion: In the space to the left, write the word or words that **BEST** complete(s) each statement.

_____ 1. One benefit of eating snacks is that they can provide an ___?___ boost between meals.

_____ 2. Wisely chosen snacks can help you eat the recommended number of servings from each of the ___?___.

_____ 3. Fruits, vegetables, and yogurt make good snacks because they contain important ___?___.

_____ 4. One negative result of frequent snacking is that ___?___ may decay.

_____ 5. People who are physically active can burn off the added ___?___ in snacks.

_____ 6. Low-calorie snacks should be chosen for someone who is on a ___?___ diet.

_____ 7. Planning ahead and having nutritious snacks on hand can help control ___?___ snacking.

_____
_____ 8. Many crackers are not as healthful as they look because they are high in ___?___ and ___?___.

_____ 9. By reading ___?___, a shopper can choose healthful snacks.

_____ 10. One advantage of popcorn as a snack is that it is a good source of ___?___.

_____ 11. Using a hot-air popper helps reduce ___?___ in popcorn.

_____ 12. Instead of salt, popcorn can be seasoned with ___?___ and ___?___.

_____
_____ 13. A bean spread is a good source of ___?___.

_____ 14. Liquid drained from beans can be used in ___?___ or ___?___.

_____

Continued on next page

_____ 15. Keeping ___?___ and ___?___ vegetables in the refrigerator makes them
ready for quick snacks.

_____

_____ 16. A healthful vegetable dip can be made by mixing seasonings with ___?___
or ___?___.

_____

_____ 17. Dipping fruit for a kabob in ___?___ will prevent it from browning.

Short Answer: Answer the following questions on the lines provided.

18. Why do snacks need to be chosen with the same care as meals?

_____

_____

_____

19. Explain how to choose healthful snacks.

_____

_____

20. What are two advantages of bringing snacks from home?

_____

_____

21. List at least six seasonings that could be used in making a vegetable dip.

_____

_____

_____

22. List at least five ideas for healthful snacks.

_____

_____

_____

Name _____ **Date** _____ **Class Hour** _____

CHAPTER 36 Snacks

Text Pages 256-261

▼ ▼ ▼ Vending Machine Choices

Directions: You and some friends have gone to the vending machine to buy snacks. In each case, your friends have narrowed the decision down to two choices. Use your knowledge of snack foods to tell them which choice would be more healthful and why.

1. Mark can't decide between a package of peanut butter cheese crackers or a chocolate and nut candy bar. Which of these is more healthful? Why?

_____

_____

_____

2. Jenna Beth is trying to decide between packages of buttered popcorn and barbecue corn chips. Which of these snacks is more healthful? Why?

_____

_____

_____

3. Raja is considering a package of devils food snack cakes and a box of chocolate covered raisins. Which of these snacks is more healthful? Why?

_____

_____

_____

4. Alana is considering a package of unsalted peanuts and a peanut-chocolate candy bar. Which is the most healthful choice? Why?

_____

_____

_____

CHAPTER 36 Snacks

Text Pages 256-261

Healthful Snacks

Directions: By using the letters below each diagram, form the names of two healthful snacks, one listed across and one listed down. The letter given is common to both snacks. Use only the letters listed.

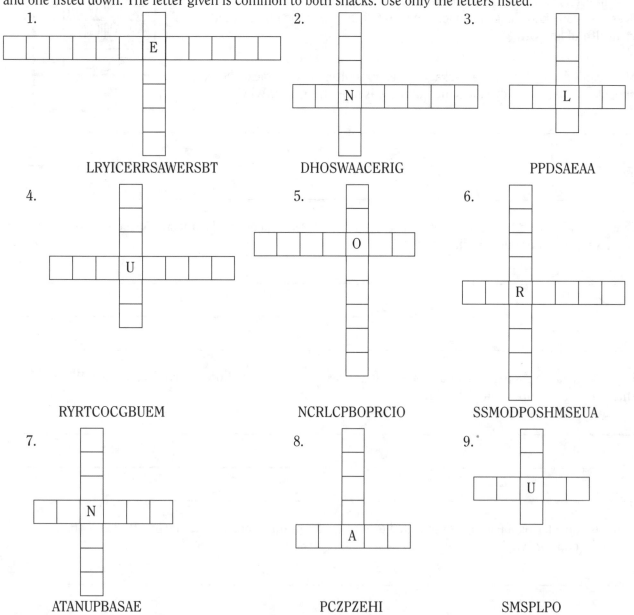

1.

E

LRYICERRSAWERSBT

2.

N

DHOSWAACERIG

3.

L

PPDSAEAA

4.

U

RYRTCOCGBUEM

5.

O

NCRLCPBOPRCIO

6.

R

SSMODPOSHMSEUA

7.

N

ATANUPBASAE

8.

A

PCZPZEHI

9.

U

SMSPLPO

10. Explain why these are healthful snacks.

_____

Study Guide

Completion: In the space to the left, write the word or words that **BEST** complete(s) each statement.

_____ 1. When quenching a thirst, the best beverage to drink is ___?___.

_____ 2. ___?___ glasses of water are needed each day for good health.

_____ 3. Milk is a healthful beverage because of the ___?___ it contains.

_____ 4. Cocoa provides calcium and phosphorus because it is made from ___?___.

_____ 5. Tomato juice provides the same ___?___ and ___?___ found in tomatoes.

_____

_____ 6. Soft drinks such as cola often contain large amounts of ___?___ or sodium.

_____ 7. A chemical that can cause nervousness or other problems is ___?___.

_____ 8. There are about ___?___ of sugar in a typical soft drink.

_____ 9. Those products labeled "juice" contain ___?___.

_____ 10. A fruit drink or punch contains ___?___, ___?___, and ___?___.

_____

_____

_____ 11. Vitamin ___?___ is added to fruit drinks labeled fortified.

_____ 12. Frozen juice concentrate must be ___?___ with water to be ready to use.

_____ 13. Beverages that are stored properly keep their ___?___ and ___?___.

_____

_____ 14. Keep juices from the ___?___ cold.

_____ 15. Most juices can be stored in a cool dry place until ___?___.

_____ 16. An open container of juice can be stored for ___?___.

Continued on next page

_____ 17. Reconstituted juices should be stored ___?___.

_____ 18. A ___?___ beverage is a hot fruit punch or juice that contains spices.

_____ 19. Special attention is needed when heating ___?___ in the microwave.

_____ 20. Beverages are heated in the microwave at ___?___% power unless the recipe says differently.

Short Answer: Answer the following questions on the lines provided.

21. What are two ways beverages are used in menu planning?

_____

22. How can beverages help meet your body's need for nutrients?

_____

_____

_____

23. Describe the nutritional advantages and disadvantages of a milk shake.

_____

_____

_____

24. Why is it a problem when children and teens choose soft drinks rather than milk?

_____

_____

_____

25. What basic ingredients can be combined for blender shakes?

_____

_____

26. Why should beverages heated in the microwave be stirred?

_____

_____

_____

_____

CHAPTER 37 Beverages   **Text Pages 262-267**

   ## Where's the Juice?

Directions: Where should a shopper look for juices in the supermarket? Match each beverage in the left column with the correct location in the supermarket from the right column. Write the letter of the location in the space provided. Each location will be used at least once.

Beverages

____ 1. Powdered orange drink mix

____ 2. Canned tomato juice

____ 3. Bottle of cranapple juice

____ 4. Frozen pineapple juice concentrate

____ 5. Fresh grapefruit juice

____ 6. Individual boxes of grape juice

____ 7. Canned vegetable juice

____ 8. Fresh orange juice

____ 9. Canned grapefruit juice

____ 10. Individual boxes of apple juice

____ 11. Frozen grape juice concentrate

____ 12. Canned apricot nectar

Supermarket Locations

A. Frozen section

B. Grocery shelves

C. Refrigerated section

Coded Messages

Directions: The following sentences contain coded terms from the chapter. Use the example and the sentences to break the code. Then decode the mystery message in number 10.

Example: <u>B</u> <u>E</u> <u>V</u> <u>E</u> <u>R</u> <u>A</u> <u>G</u> <u>E</u> <u>S</u>
        Y V E V I Z T V H

1. Sometimes a mixture of fruit juices is called a __ __ __ __ __   __ __ __ __ __ .
               U I F R G   K F M X S

2. A beverage high in potassium and vitamin C is __ __ __ __ __   __ __ __ __ __ .
            L I Z M T V   Q F R X V

3. The only way to know exactly what is in a beverage container is to

__ __ __ __   __ __ __   __ __ __ __ __ .
I V Z W   G S V   O Z Y V O

4. Coffee and tea contain __ __ __ __ __ __ __ __ that can cause nervousness.
                 X Z U U V R M V

5. Drinking __ __ __ __ __ is the best way to quench a thirst.
         D Z G V I

6. A product that contains some juice with water and sweeteners is called a

__ __ __ __   __ __ __ __ __ .
U I F R G   W I R M P

7. Drinking __ __ __ __ provides vitamins A and D.
        N R O P

8. Regular soft drinks contain lots of __ __ __ __ __ .
               H F T Z I

9. Until you are ready to use them, keep fruit juice concentrates __ __ __ __ __ __ .
                             U I L A V M

10. __ __ __ __ __ __ __ __ __   __ __ __ __ __   __ __ __ __ __ __ __ __ __
   X Z I V U F O O B   X S L L H V   Y V E V I Z T V H

__ __ __   __ __ __ __   __ __ __ __ __ __   __ __ __   __ __ __ __
U L I   T L L W   S V Z O G S   Z M W   T L L W

__ __ __ __ __ __ __ __ .
M F G I R G R L M

Study Guide

Completion: In the space to the left, write the word or words that **BEST** complete(s) each statement.

_____ 1. The appearance, texture, and flavor of baked products are due to ___?___ reactions that occur during baking.

_____ 2. The structure of baked goods is provided by proteins and starch in ___?___.

_____ 3. Baking powder is an example of a(n) ___?___.

_____ 4. ___?___ work with flour to form the structure of baked products.

_____ 5. Products are made rich and tender by ___?___ and ___?___.

_____

_____ 6. The ingredients in a mixture are often held together by ___?___.

_____ 7. A mixture thick enough to be shaped by hand or cut into shapes is ___?___.

_____ 8. A mixture thin enough to be dropped or poured is ___?___.

_____ 9. An elastic substance called ___?___ is formed by the protein in flour.

_____ 10. Sifting, creaming, or beating traps ___?___ in the mixture.

_____ 11. High temperatures cause water to turn to ___?___, a leavening agent.

_____ 12. Baking soda and baking powder are ___?___ leavening agents.

_____ 13. ___?___ gas is formed when baking soda is combined with an acid.

_____ 14. Baking soda combined with a dry acid is known as ___?___.

_____ 15. A microscopic plant known as ___?___ releases gas as it grows.

_____ 16. Heat causes gas or air to ___?___ when batter or dough is baked.

_____ 17. Using a pan too ___?___ may cause the product to be thin or not brown.

_____ 18. If the oven ___?___ is too low, the baked product may be soggy and sunken.

Continued on next page

_____ 19. Recipe writers assume that shiny ___?___ pans will be used for baking.

_____ 20. ___?___ the oven will allow the mixture to begin baking immediately.

_____ 21. Using ___?___ with grease can make a product easier to remove from the pan.

_____ 22. Wiping off the pan will remove ___?___ that can burn easily in the oven.

Short Answer: Answer the following questions on the lines provided.

23. Explain how baked goods such as breads and cakes are similar. How are they different?

_____

_____

_____

24. Describe how leavening agents work and why they are important.

_____

_____

_____

25. Identify at least three purposes for eggs in a baked product.

_____

_____

_____

26. What are the chemical reactions during baking dependent upon?

_____

_____

27. Why should you use the exact ingredients called for when baking?

_____

_____

28. Explain how to flour a greased pan.

_____

_____

CHAPTER **38** Principles of Baking   **Text Pages 268-275**

     A File for Baking

Directions: The numbers beneath the answer blanks below correspond to the numbers on the drawers of the filing cabinet. Find the file drawer that corresponds with the numbers below the blank. Then figure out which of the letters on the file drawer you need to spell the correct word. Write the letter in the appropriate space. If you think you know the answer from the clue alone, use the file drawer numbers to check your accuracy.

ABC 1
DEF 2
GHIJ 3
KLMN 4
OPQR 5
STUV 6
WXYZ 7

1. An ingredient that provides air or gas that makes a baked product rise.

   __ __ __ __ __ __ __ __ __   __ __ __ __ __
   4 2 1 6 2 4 3 4 3   1 3 2 4 6

2. An ingredient that gives flavor to a baked product.

   __ __ __ __ __ __ __ __ __
   6 7 2 2 6 2 4 2 5

3. A utensil used to cool baked products.

   __ __ __ __   __ __ __ __
   7 3 5 2   5 1 1 4

4. A mixture of ingredients thin enough to be dropped from a spoon.

   __ __ __ __ __ __
   1 1 6 6 2 5

5. An ingredient that provides protein and starch in baked products.

   __ __ __ __ __
   2 4 5 6 5

6. An ingredient recommended for greasing pans.

   __ __ __ __ __ __ __ __   __ __ __ __ __ __ __ __ __
   6 4 6 1 4 6 2 2   6 3 5 5 6 2 4 3 4 3

7. An example of a chemical leavening agent.

   __ __ __ __ __ __   __ __ __ __ __ __
   1 1 4 3 4 3   5 5 7 2 2 5

Continued on next page

8. These ingredients help make products rich and tender.

¯¯ ¯¯ ¯¯ ¯¯   ¯¯ ¯¯ ¯¯   ¯¯ ¯¯ ¯¯ ¯¯
2 1 6 6   1 4 2   5 3 4 6

9. An example of an acid food often used with baking soda for leavening.

¯¯ ¯¯ ¯¯ ¯¯ ¯¯ ¯¯ ¯¯ ¯¯ ¯¯
1 6 6 6 2 5 4 3 4 4

10. This ingredient helps bind ingredients together.

¯¯ ¯¯ ¯¯ ¯¯
2 3 3 6

11. These affect the final appearance, texture, and flavor of baked products.

¯¯ ¯¯ ¯¯ ¯¯ ¯¯ ¯¯ ¯¯ ¯¯   ¯¯ ¯¯ ¯¯ ¯¯ ¯¯ ¯¯ ¯¯ ¯¯
1 3 2 4 3 1 1 4   5 2 1 1 6 3 5 4 6

12. An ingredient that makes possible the chemical changes that take place in baked products.

¯¯ ¯¯ ¯¯ ¯¯ ¯¯ ¯¯
4 3 5 6 3 2

13. A microscopic plant that acts as a leavening agent.

¯¯ ¯¯ ¯¯ ¯¯ ¯¯
7 2 1 6 6

14. A mixture of ingredients thick enough to be shaped by hand.

¯¯ ¯¯ ¯¯ ¯¯ ¯¯
2 5 6 3 3

15. An elastic substance formed by the protein in flour.

¯¯ ¯¯ ¯¯ ¯¯ ¯¯ ¯¯
3 4 6 6 2 4

16. A leavening agent created by heat and water.

¯¯ ¯¯ ¯¯ ¯¯ ¯¯
6 6 2 1 4

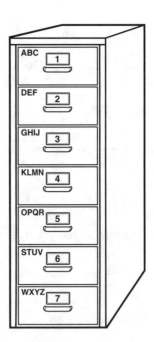

ABC 1
DEF 2
GHIJ 3
KLMN 4
OPQR 5
STUV 6
WXYZ 7

Name _____ **Date** _____ **Class Hour** _____

CHAPTER 38 Principles of Baking

Text Pages 268-275

Analyzing Recipe Ingredients

Directions: In the chart on the next page, the seven categories of ingredients commonly used in baking are listed on the left. Write the purpose of each ingredient in the spaces provided. Then read the ingredient list for Pineapple-Pecan Bread. Write the name of the ingredients that is (are) an example(s) of the ingredient category in the recipe.

Pineapple-Pecan Bread

½ cup (125 mL) brown sugar

¼ cup (50 mL) butter or margarine

1 egg

2 cups (500 mL) all-purpose flour

1 tsp. (5 mL) baking soda

⅓ cup (75 mL) frozen orange
  juice concentrate, thawed

3 Tbsp. (45 mL) water

1 8.5-oz. (240-g) can crushed pineapple,
  undrained

1 tsp. (5 mL) vanilla

½ cup (125 mL) chopped pecans

Continued on next page

Ingredient Category	Purpose of Ingredient in Recipe	Example(s) of Ingredient Category in Pineapple-Pecan Bread
Flour	1.	8.
Leavening Agent	2.	9.
Liquid	3.	10.
Fat/Oil	4.	11.
Sweetener	5.	12.
Eggs	6.	13.
Flavoring	7.	14.

CHAPTER 38 Principles of Baking   **Text Pages 268-275**

Preparing to Bake

Directions: Assume you are preparing to bake a layer cake. The recipe tells you to prepare the baking pans. Listed below are the steps to follow when preparing a cake pan for baking. Place a 1 in the blank to the left of the first step in preparing a cake pan. Place a 2 in the blank to the left of the second step. Continue until all steps are numbered in order.

_____ 1. Hold the pan in both hands, gently turning it to spread the flour evenly over the bottom and sides of the pan.

_____ 2. Using waxed paper or a paper towel, spread shortening in a thin, even layer over the bottom and sides of the pan.

_____ 3. Turn the pan upside down.

_____ 4. Sprinkle about 1 tablespoon (15 mL) of flour over the pan.

_____ 5. Hold the pan over a large piece of waxed paper.

_____ 6. Tap the pan gently to remove excess flour.

_____ 7. Tap the pan gently to spread the flour.

Directions: The cake recipe you are using says that the cake batter can be baked in two round 8 x 1 1/2 inch (20 x 4 cm) cake pans or in one rectangular 9 x 13 x 2 inch (23 x 33 x 5 cm) cake pan. On the oven rack drawings below, draw the placement of the cake pans for baking using both the round pans and the rectangular pan.

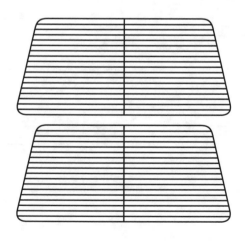

Round Cake Pans

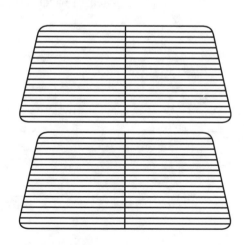

Rectangular Cake Pan

CHAPTER 38 **Principles of Baking** **Text Pages 268-275**

   STEPS to Baking Success

Directions: Five important steps in successful baking are listed on the stair steps below. On the lines provided, explain why each step is important in baking success.

5. Use the correct oven temperature. Why?

_____

_____

4. Use the correct type and size of pan. Why?

_____

_____

3. Follow the directions in the recipe. Why?

_____

_____

2. Measure accurately. Why?

_____

_____

1. Use the exact ingredients called for in the recipe. Why?

_____

_____

Study Guide

Completion: In the space to the left, write the word or words that **BEST** complete(s) each statement.

_____ 1. ___?___ require less preparation time than yeast breads.

_____ 2. ___?___ is usually used as a leavening agent in quick breads.

_____ 3. When quick bread are made with ___?___ flour, they provide fiber.

_____ 4. Use ___?___ flour if the recipe does not call for a specific type of flour.

_____ 5. Flour and sweeteners should both be stored in ___?___ containers.

_____ 6. White table sugar is known as ___?___ sugar.

_____ 7. ___?___ is added to white table sugar to make brown sugar.

_____ 8. Powdered sugar is also known as ___?___ sugar.

_____ 9. The type of fat that is highest in saturated fat is ___?___.

_____ 10. Prepared quick breads should be wrapped well and stored at ___?___ temperature.

_____ 11. The ___?___ and ___?___ methods are the most common methods for quick breads.

_____

_____ 12. ___?___ batter should have a lumpy texture.

_____ 13. When a muffin has tunnels, it is a result of ___?___.

_____ 14. Biscuits have a ___?___ texture because of the biscuit method of mixing.

_____ 15. Working or pressing dough with your hands is known as ___?___.

_____ 16. Kneading helps form ___?___, the elastic structure of the dough.

_____ 17. Once biscuit dough is kneaded, the biscuits should be ___?___ and ___?___.

_____

Continued on next page

_____ 18. Baked biscuits should have ___?___ sides and lightly browned tops.

_____ 19. Yeast bread dough needs to rise for about ___?___ before it is shaped.

_____ 20. When microwaving muffins, fill the muffin cups about ___?___ full.

_____ 21. Microwave quick breads do not ___?___ like those made conventionally.

_____ 22. Quick breads can be reheated in the microwave at ___?___% power.

Short Answer: Answer the following questions on the lines provided.

23. List the nutrients typically found in quick breads.

_____

_____

_____

24. What determines how healthful quick breads are?

_____

_____

_____

25. Explain the muffin method of mixing ingredients.

_____

_____

_____

26. Name at least two ways to tell if muffins or quick bread loaves are done baking.

_____

_____

27. Describe how to prepare biscuit dough.

_____

_____

_____

CHAPTER 39 Quick Breads   **Text Pages 276-283**

   Mixing Methods

Directions: The steps in the muffin and biscuit methods of making quick breads are mixed up in the muffins and biscuits below. Identify which step belongs to which mixing method and write the steps in the proper order on the blanks below.

Mix dry ingredients together in a bowl.

Cut shortening into dry ingredients.

Sift dry ingredients together in bowl.

Mix liquid ingredients together in a bowl.

Mix batter just long enough to moisten dry ingredients.

Add liquid to the crumb-like mixture.

Mix to make a soft dough.

Add liquid ingredients to the dry ingredients.

Muffin Method	Biscuit Method
1.	1.
2.	2.
3.	3.
4.	4.

CHAPTER 39 Quick Breads   Text Pages 276-283

Quick Bread Combinations

Directions: Put together letter combinations from the list below to form terms from Chapter 39. Use the clues and the letter combinations to help you discover the terms. Cross off the letter combinations in the list as you use them.

List of Letter Combinations

AD	AVE	BIS	CA	CO	CU
ED	ELS	ER	ES	FIN	FLE
IT	IUM	KNE	LA	LC	LE
MO	MUF	NN	NS	PO	RED
SS	TU	VE	WAF	WD	

Clues   **Terms**

1. To work or press dough with the hands.   _____

2. A type of quick bread.   _____

3. A method for mixing quick breads.   _____

4. What baking powder does for quick breads.   _____

5. Mineral in quick bread provided by milk.   _____

6. A result of overmixing.   _____

7. The kind of container in which flour is stored. _____

8. A method for mixing quick breads.   _____

9. An ingredient in brown sugar.   _____

10. Sugar that has a fine texture.   _____

CHAPTER **40** Cookies, Cakes, and Pies   **Text Pages 285-293**

 Study Guide

Completion: In the space to the left, write the word or words that **BEST** complete(s) each statement.

_____ 1. Eat few cookies, cakes, and pies; they have ___?___, ___?___, and ___?___.

_____

_____

_____ 2. Angel food cake and gingersnaps are fairly low in ___?___.

_____ 3. Cookies, cakes, and pies use the same basic ___?___ as other baked goods.

_____ 4. ___?___ are usually added to packaged cake and cookie mixes before baking.

_____ 5. Cream pies and cakes with cream fillings should be stored ___?___.

_____ 6. ___?___ will grow quickly in unrefrigerated custards and cream pies.

_____ 7. The six basic types of cookies are different in ___?___.

_____ 8. Brownies are an example of ___?___ cookies.

_____ 9. Chocolate chip cookies are a popular ___?___ cookie.

_____ 10. ___?___ cookies are shaped by hand from a stiff dough.

_____ 11. Pushing dough through a cookie press will form ___?___ cookies.

_____ 12. Dough cut into shapes with cookie cutters makes ___?___ cookies.

_____ 13. Dip utensils in ___?___ to prevent dough from sticking to them.

_____ 14. ___?___ cakes contain baking powder or baking soda as a leavener.

_____ 15. When a(n) ___?___ cake is baked it will be pulled away from the sides.

_____ 16. ___?___ cakes are cooled in the pan in which they were baked.

_____ 17. A topping made from sugar and beaten egg white is a(n) ___?___.

Continued on next page

_____ 18. A fruit pie with only a top crust is called a(n) ___?___ pie.

_____ 19. ___?___ pans should be used when microwaving cookies and cakes.

_____ 20. To microwave a one-crust pie ___?___ the crust before adding the filling.

_____ 21. ___?___ pies need to be baked in the conventional oven.

_____ 22. Microwave cookies will look ___?___ when they are done.

Short Answer: Answer the following questions on the lines provided.

23. How can a plan for healthful eating include cookies, cakes, and pies when these products are high in sugar, fat, and calories?

_____

_____

_____

24. How should you store soft cookies? Crisp cookies? Why?

_____

_____

_____

25. What will happen if you sprinkle too much flour on the rolling pin when rolling out cookies?

_____

26. Explain how to remove a cake from the pan.

_____

_____

_____

27. Explain how to prepare a crumb pie crust.

_____

_____

_____

CHAPTER 40 Cookies, Cakes, and Pies   Text Pages 285-293

Problem Solvers

Directions: Read the situations below. Answer the questions on the lines provided.

1. Dale bought a ready-made graham cracker pie crust. How will he know how to store it?

   _____

   _____

   _____

2. Carlotta is on a low-fat diet. She allows herself one dessert treat a week. What are two sweets that are relatively low in fat?

   _____

   _____

   _____

3. Paul wants to make a pie to serve his friends, but he only has an hour before they arrive. All the recipes he checks take too long. What could he do?

   _____

   _____

   _____

   _____

4. Kamilla is making rolled gingerbread cookies, but the dough keeps sticking to her rolling pin and the cookie cutter. What should she do?

   _____

   _____

   _____

   _____

Continued on next page

5. Ho-Choog made oatmeal cookies. Some were thick and chewy while others were thin, crisp, and very brown. What could Ho-Choog have done to prevent this?

_____

_____

_____

_____

6. Lita was making a batch of molded lemon cookies. She was refilling the baking sheet as soon as she removed the baked cookies. Many of her cookies were very spread out and thin. What could have prevented this?

_____

_____

_____

_____

7. Andre made an angel food cake. When he went to take it out of the pan, it had fallen and was very thin. How could he have prevented this from happening?

_____

_____

_____

_____

8. Minh baked a pan of brownies in a square pan in the microwave. The corners were burned and hard and couldn't be eaten. Why did this happen? How could Minh have prevented it?

_____

_____

_____

_____

Discovering Food and Nutrition Student Workbook Protected by Copyright ©

CHAPTER 40 Cookies, Cakes, and Pies

Hidden Treats

Directions: The puzzle below contains 20 "treats" from the chapter. Use the clues on the next page and the puzzle below to discover the hidden treats. Write each treat on the blank to the left of the clue that describes it and circle the treat in the puzzle. The treats may appear backwards, forwards, horizontally, or vertically.

```
N  Z  T  I  R  P  S  N  S  P  O  N  G  E
O  C  O  T  I  U  R  F  T  H  R  E  N  A
F  U  Q  O  L  L  F  W  S  B  Y  O  I  N
F  R  I  R  D  Y  I  A  U  M  A  A  D  G
I  L  B  R  G  E  G  D  R  U  B  F  D  E
H  S  R  A  S  N  B  E  C  R  C  E  U  L
C  H  O  C  O  L  A  T  E  C  H  I  P  F
U  P  W  P  A  S  R  T  N  D  O  S  T  O
S  Z  N  U  I  V  M  A  O  K  C  D  K  O
T  C  I  C  B  R  Y  E  L  L  O  W  X  D
A  M  E  R  I  N  G  U  E  E  L  P  P  A
R  J  S  E  P  O  O  H  Z  D  A  T  Y  N
D  N  M  A  L  V  I  P  A  S  T  R  Y  G
J  C  E  M  A  S  H  O  R  T  E  N  E  D
```

Continued on next page

_____ 1. A popular kind of drop cookie.

_____ 2. A kind of cookie that is low in fat.

_____ 3. This kind of cake would provide vitamin A.

_____ 4. This kind of pie needs to be refrigerated.

_____ 5. A kind of unshortened cake.

_____ 6. A kind of shortened cake.

_____ 7. This kind of cake is cooled upside down in the pan.

_____ 8. An example of a two-crust pie.

_____ 9. An example of a one-crust pie.

_____ 10. This is whipped to make a topping for a one-crust pie.

_____ 11. A mixture of egg whites and sugar used on one-crust pies.

_____ 12. The most commonly used pie crust.

_____ 13. A kind of crust made from crushed graham crackers.

_____ 14. The type of filling found in cream pies.

_____ 15. The most popular kind of pie filling.

_____ 16. A kind of fruit pie made with gelatin.

_____ 17. A kind of pressed cookie.

_____ 18. A kind of cake that can be adapted for the microwave.

_____ 19. A kind of pie that can be prepared in the microwave.

_____ 20. An example of a bar cookie.

CHAPTER 40 Cookies, Cakes, and Pies   Text Pages 285-293

Sweet Treat Match Ups

Directions: Match each description or example in the left column with the correct type of cookie from the right column. Write the letter of the type of cookie in the space provided. Each type of cookie will be used at least once.

Description or Example

_____ 1. Sliced from a long roll of chilled dough.

_____ 2. Peanut butter cookies.

_____ 3. Shaped from a stiff dough with a cookie press.

_____ 4. Shaped by dropping batter on a baking sheet.

_____ 5. Made with cookie cutters from stiff dough.

_____ 6. Brownies.

_____ 7. Spritz cookies.

_____ 8. Baked in a square or rectangular pan and cut into shapes.

_____ 9. Shaped by hand from a stiff dough.

_____ 10. Sugar cookies.

Type of Cookie

A. Bar

B. Drop

C. Molded

D. Pressed

E. Refrigerator

F. Rolled

Continued on next page

Directions: Match each description or example in the left column with the correct type of pie from the right column. Write the letter of the type of pie in the space provided. Each type of pie will be used at least once.

Description or Example

_____ 11. Coconut cream

_____ 12. Lemon meringue

_____ 13. Has a top crust with a fruit filling.

_____ 14. Has a filling between a top and bottom crust.

_____ 15. Blueberry pie.

_____ 16. Has a bottom crust with a filling.

Type of Pie

A. Two-crust pie

B. One-crust pie

C. Deep-dish pie

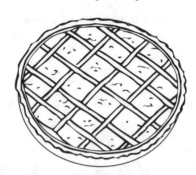

Directions: Match each description or example in the left column with the correct types of cake from the right column. Write the letter of the type of pie in the space provided.

Description or Example

_____ 17. A cake that does not contain fat or oil.

_____ 18. A cake that contains fat, such as shortening or margarine.

_____ 19. A cake that contains baking powder or soda for leavening.

_____ 20. A cake that is baked in a tube pan.

Type of Cake

A. Shortened cakes

B. Unshortened cakes